Mathematical Thinking
Level A
MULTILEVEL MATH PRACTICE TO IMPROVE STRATEGIC THINKING AND TEST-TAKING SKILLS

Written by
Trisha Callella

Editor: Alaska Hults
Illustrator: Corbin Hillam
Cover Illustrator: Rick Grayson
Designer: Moonhee Pak
Cover Designer: Moonhee Pak
Art Director: Tom Cochrane
Project Director: Carolea Williams

© 2001 Creative Teaching Press, Inc., Huntington Beach, CA 92649
Reproduction of activities in any manner for use in the classroom and not for commercial sale is permissible.
Reproduction of these materials for an entire school or for a school system is strictly prohibited.

Table of Contents

Introduction 3
How to Use This Book 4

Problem Sets

Patterns 5
Section Answers 22

Data Analysis and Probability 23
Section Answers 40

Geometry and Spatial Relationships 41
Section Answers 58

Logic and Critical Thinking 59
Section Answers 76

Measurement 77
Section Answers 94

Mathematical Reasoning 95
Section Answers 112

Introduction

Mathematical Thinking focuses on six math standards that children rarely experience in a multiple-choice, timed-testing format. For example, children often build patterns with connecting cubes (or similar toys such as LEGO®s), but they often fail to understand how to identify in a multiple-choice format the answer that shows a missing element in a pattern. The problems in *Mathematical Thinking* give children the opportunity to practice specific math concepts in a multiple-choice format.

Mathematical Thinking contains in a standardized-test format 15 problem sets (a page of three problems) for each math standard. The first page of each *Mathematical Thinking* section provides a brief definition of the targeted concept, one or two ideas for supporting that concept in an interactive way, and test-taking tips that children can use to improve their performance on multiple-choice tests. The second page of each section is a chart that cross-references the specific math concepts that children need to solve each problem set. An answer key is provided at the end of each section.

Each problem set has three levels of difficulty. The ● problem introduces the concept, the ▲ problem provides an opportunity to independently practice the concept, and the ■ problem provides a more challenging application of the concept. Each problem has an Extend the Thinking question that encourages children to either build on the information in the problem or to communicate their reasoning. Because the purpose of the problems is to help children build test-taking skills and to provide practice with the math standards, it is helpful to do the problem sets in a whole-class setting. Refer to How to Use This Book (page 4) to decide how to implement the problem sets in a way that fits your teaching style and math curriculum.

How to Use This Book

Choose a problem set, and photocopy it for each child. Make an overhead transparency of the problem set to facilitate class discussion. Children may not be able to decode some of the mathematical terms, so read aloud the first problem, and discuss it as a class. Demonstrate how to fill in the answer bubbles, and then have children work together (in pairs or small groups) on the ● problem. Be sure to have them complete on the back of their paper the Extend the Thinking problem. Then, refer to the answer page at the end of each section, and discuss the solution as a class. Invite children to share how they solved the problem as well as the actual solution. Then, either assign both the ▲ and ■ problems for children to work on individually, or have each child solve a developmentally appropriate problem (steering more fluent math students toward the ■ problem). After children have completed their work, discuss both problems as a class.

Keep in mind that the purpose of the problem sets is to teach children how to solve problems in a multiple-choice format. If the class seems to be struggling with a specific concept, set aside the problems, teach the concept in your usual math instruction, and then return to the problems when children are ready.

Present problem sets within each section sequentially. You may choose to have children complete a given section or one problem set from each section (to cover up to five concepts in one week). At the start of each week, introduce one test-taking strategy (from the first page of each section), and encourage children to practice that strategy during the week. Focus on a general tip, such as getting necessary rest the night before a test, or on specific concepts, such as how to solve analogy problems.

4   *How to Use This Book*

Patterns

The *Level A* Patterns standards require children to

- create patterns with shapes, designs, objects, and numbers
- extend patterns
- identify a part that is missing from a pattern
- apply the concept of a pattern to a real-life situation
- notice number patterns that occur in real life

Pattern Pairs

Divide the class into pairs. Give one child in each pair a plastic bag filled with pattern blocks or snap cubes. Ask that child to make a pattern that repeats at least three times. When the child is finished, have the other partner extend the pattern. Have partners switch roles so each child has a chance to make a pattern and extend a pattern.

Musical Patterns

In advance, locate a xylophone with different-colored keys. Give each child a set of snap cubes in the same colors as the xylophone keys. Have children make a pattern and then play on the xylophone the tune that matches the colors of their pattern so children can both see and hear the pattern they created. Store the xylophone and a bag of snap cubes at a learning center so that children can have pattern fun on their own.

TEST-TAKING TIPS FOR CHILDREN

✔ Read the directions carefully and watch for a change in directions—directions may vary within the same section of a test.

✔ Read all the choices even if you think you've found the right answer.

✔ Treat each choice as a true or false statement. Select the answer that is true.

TEACHING TIP FOR THIS SECTION

Tell children that they can sometimes more easily solve a pattern problem, especially a non-numerical pattern problem, if they describe aloud each element. For example, the ● problem on page 7 can be read *bug, bird, bug, bird, bug,* which helps children hear that the next element should be *bird (b)*.

→ Answers are on page 22.

Concepts: Patterns

Math Concept	page 7	page 8	page 9	page 10	page 11	page 12	page 13	page 14	page 15	page 16	page 17	page 18	page 19	page 20	page 21
Patterns	X	X	X	X	X	X	X	X	X	X	X	X	X	X	X
Shapes		X			X	X			X	X	X	X			
Number Sense			X	X											
Spatial Relationships					X	X						X	X	X	
Critical Thinking							X	X			X	X			
Multiplication														X	
Division															X

Problem Set

6 Patterns

1 2 1 2 1 2 ___

Which number comes next in the pattern?

(a) 2   (b) 1   (c) 7   (d) 0

EXTEND THE THINKING: Use these numbers to make a new pattern.

1 2 2 1 2 2 1 2 2 ___

Which number comes next in the pattern?

(a) 7   (b) 1   (c) 4   (d) 3

EXTEND THE THINKING: Use these numbers to make a new pattern.

1 2 3 1 2 3 ___

Which number comes next in the pattern?

(a) 8   (b) 0   (c) 1   (d) 2

EXTEND THE THINKING: Use these numbers to make a new pattern.

Patterns 9

8   7   6   5   4   ___

Which number comes next in the pattern?

(a) 5   (b) 3   (c) 1   (d) 0

EXTEND THE THINKING: What are the next 3 numbers?

3   2   1   3   2   ___

Which number comes next in the pattern?

(a) 7   (b) 1   (c) 4   (d) 3

EXTEND THE THINKING: What are the next 3 numbers?

3   3   3   2   2   1   3   3   ___

Which number comes next in the pattern?

(a) 2   (b) 0   (c) 1   (d) 3

EXTEND THE THINKING: What are the next 3 numbers?

10   Patterns

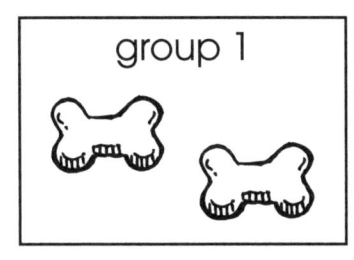

| group 1 | group 2 | group 3 |

Which group is different?

ⓐ group 1   ⓑ group 2   ⓒ group 3   ⓓ none of these choices

EXTEND THE THINKING: Why is that group different?

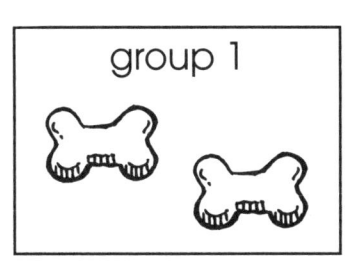

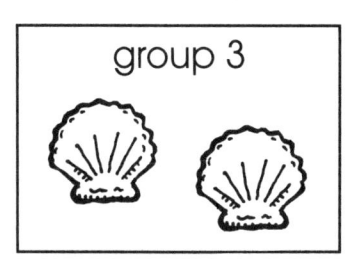

| group 1 | group 2 | group 3 |

Which group is different?

ⓐ group 1   ⓑ group 2   ⓒ group 3   ⓓ none of these choices

EXTEND THE THINKING: Why is that group different?

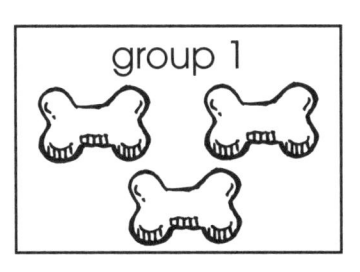

| group 1 | group 2 | group 3 |

Which group is different?

ⓐ group 1   ⓑ group 2   ⓒ group 3   ⓓ none of these choices

EXTEND THE THINKING: Why is that group different?

Patterns 13

Which picture is different?

(a) 1   (b) 2   (c) 3   (d) none of these choices

EXTEND THE THINKING: Why is that picture different?

Which picture is different?

(a) 1   (b) 2   (c) 3   (d) none of these choices

EXTEND THE THINKING: Why is that picture different?

Which picture is different?

(a) 1   (b) 2   (c) 3   (d) none of these choices

EXTEND THE THINKING: Why is that picture different?

Patterns

○ □ ○ □ __ □

Which shape is missing in the pattern?

(a) ○   (b) ⬡   (c) □   (d) △

EXTEND THE THINKING: Use these shapes to make a new pattern.

△ △ □ △ △ □ __ △

Which shape is missing in the pattern?

(a) △   (b) ⬡   (c) □   (d) ○

EXTEND THE THINKING: Use these shapes to make a new pattern.

○ □ △ ○ __ △ ○

Which shape is missing in the pattern?

(a) ⬡   (b) ○   (c) △   (d) □

EXTEND THE THINKING: Use these shapes to make a new pattern.

Patterns 15

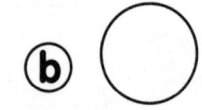

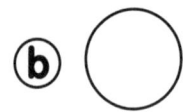

△ ○ △ △ ○ ___ ○ △

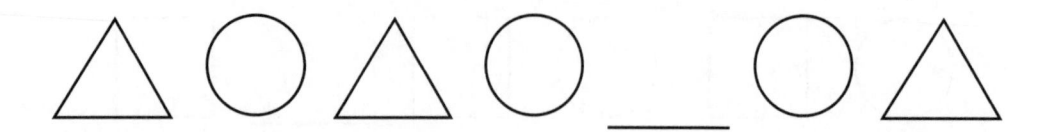

Which shape is missing in the pattern?

(a) △   (b) ○   (c) ▽   (d) ⬡

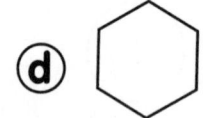

EXTEND THE THINKING: Use these shapes to make a new pattern.

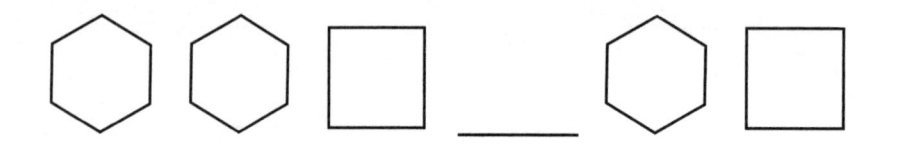

⬡ ⬡ ☐ ___ ⬡ ☐

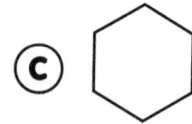

Which shape is missing in the pattern?

(a) ☐   (b) ○   (c) ⬡   (d) △

EXTEND THE THINKING: Use these shapes to make a new pattern.

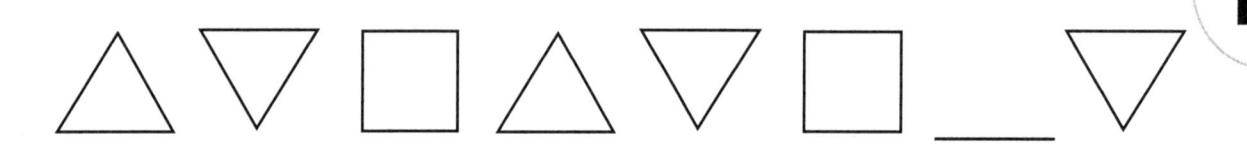

△ ▽ ☐ △ ▽ ☐ ___ ▽

Which shape is missing in the pattern?

(a) ○   (b) ☐   (c) ▽   (d) △

EXTEND THE THINKING: Use these shapes to make a new pattern.

16 Patterns

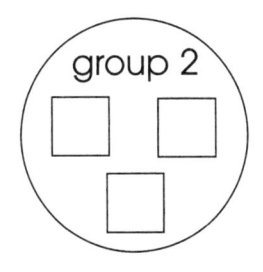

group 1   group 2   group 3

Which group does not belong?

ⓐ group 1   ⓑ group 2   ⓒ group 3   ⓓ none of these choices

EXTEND THE THINKING: Tell how that group is different from the other groups.

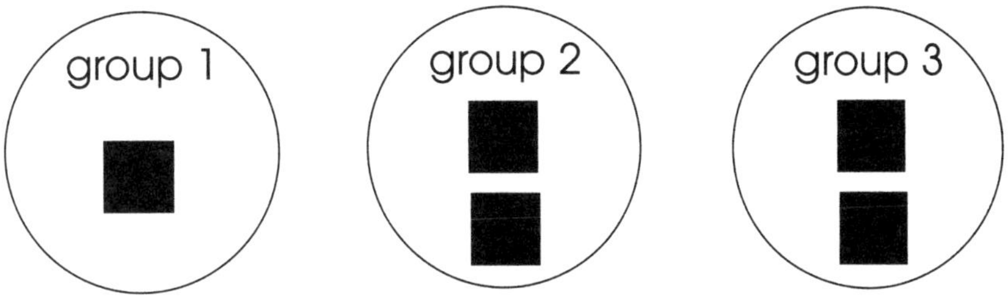

group 1   group 2   group 3

Which group does not belong?

ⓐ group 1   ⓑ group 2   ⓒ group 3   ⓓ none of these choices

EXTEND THE THINKING: Tell how that group is different from the other groups.

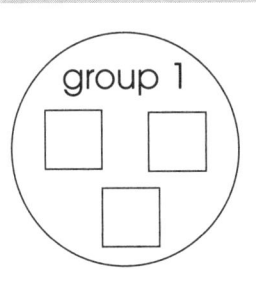

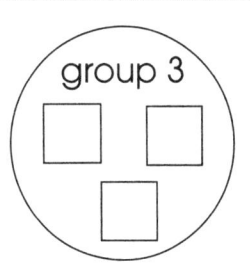

group 1   group 2   group 3

Which group does not belong?

ⓐ group 1   ⓑ group 2   ⓒ group 3   ⓓ none of these choices

EXTEND THE THINKING: Tell how that group is different from the other groups.

Patterns 17

Which shape does not belong with the others in the group?

ⓐ △   ⓑ ○   ⓒ □   ⓓ ⬡

EXTEND THE THINKING: Tell how that shape is different.

Which shape does not belong with the others in the group?

ⓐ ◇   ⓑ ⬭   ⓒ ▭   ⓓ ▯

EXTEND THE THINKING: Tell how that shape is different.

Which shape does not belong with the others in the group?

ⓐ □   ⓑ ◇   ⓒ ▭   ⓓ ⬡

EXTEND THE THINKING: Tell how that shape is different.

18 Patterns

Which design comes next?

ⓐ　　ⓑ　　ⓒ　　ⓓ

EXTEND THE THINKING: Tell why that design comes next.

Which design comes next?

ⓐ　　ⓑ　　ⓒ　　ⓓ

EXTEND THE THINKING: Tell why that design comes next.

Which design comes next?

ⓐ　　ⓑ　　ⓒ　　ⓓ

EXTEND THE THINKING: Tell why that design comes next.

Patterns   19

If 1 chick has 2 legs, how many legs do 2 chicks have?

(a) 2   (b) 4   (c) 1   (d) 10

EXTEND THE THINKING: Tell how you solved the problem.

If 1 chick has 2 legs, how many legs do 3 chicks have?

(a) 6   (b) 4   (c) 1   (d) 10

EXTEND THE THINKING: Tell how you solved the problem.

If 1 chick has 2 legs, how many legs do 5 chicks have?

(a) 2   (b) 4   (c) 1   (d) 10

EXTEND THE THINKING: Tell how you solved the problem.

You see only the ears of bunnies playing in the flowers. If 2 ears are showing, how many bunnies are playing?

(a) 1   (b) 3   (c) 4   (d) 10

EXTEND THE THINKING: Tell how you solved the problem.

You see only the ears of bunnies playing in the flowers. If 4 ears are showing, how many bunnies are playing?

(a) 1   (b) 10   (c) 4   (d) 2

EXTEND THE THINKING: Tell how you solved the problem.

You see only the ears of bunnies playing in the flowers. If 10 ears are showing, how many bunnies are playing?

(a) 1   (b) 10   (c) 5   (d) 2

EXTEND THE THINKING: Tell how you solved the problem.

Section Answers
Patterns

Correct answers are shaded.

	page 7	page 8	page 9	page 10	page 11
○	a **b** c d	**a** b c d	a **b** c d	a **b** c d	a **b** c d
△	a **b** c d	a b c **d**	**a** b c d	a **b** c d	a b **c** d
□	a b **c** d	a **b** c d	a b **c** d	a b c **d**	a **b** c d

	page 12	page 13	page 14	page 15	page 16
○	a b **c** d	a b **c** d	a **b** c d	**a** b c d	**a** b c d
△	**a** b c d	a **b** c d	a b **c** d	**a** b c d	a b **c** d
□	a b **c** d	a **b** c d	a **b** c d	a b c **d**	a b c **d**

	page 17	page 18	page 19	page 20	page 21
○	a **b** c d	a **b** c d	**a** b c d	a **b** c d	**a** b c d
△	**a** b c d	a **b** c d	a b c **d**	**a** b c d	a b c **d**
□	a **b** c d	a b c **d**	a b c **d**	a b c **d**	a b **c** d

22 *Patterns*

Data Analysis and Probability

The *Level A* Data Analysis and Probability standards require children to

- collect, compare, contrast, and analyze data (information)
- identify the important and unimportant information in a problem
- make assumptions and inferences based on information
- recognize and apply the likelihood of outcomes based on number, size, and application (the manner in which the elements are arranged or chosen)
- understand and apply the idea of probability

Interpreting Graphs

Create graphs that display information your class can interpret. Ask children
What information does the graph tell me?
How many people participated?
What was the most/least . . . ? Why?
If ___ more people had chosen _____, how would the results be different?

Exploring Probability

Draw the same symbol on the back of five index cards and a different symbol on the back of two index cards. Draw a two-column chart on the board or a piece of chart paper. Tape one card with the first symbol at the top of the first column and one card with the second symbol at the top of the second column. Show children the remaining five cards, and place them in a box. Ask children to predict which card they are most likely to choose. Then, have children take turns choosing a card from the box. After each child's turn, record the chosen card by writing a check mark in the corresponding column, and then place the card back in the box. Repeat this activity for as many times as is necessary to demonstrate that the first (more common) symbol is more likely to be chosen.

✏️ TEST-TAKING TIPS FOR CHILDREN

✔ Use common sense. Disregard the obviously incorrect choices; then consider the remaining answers to find the "best" choice.

✔ Don't rush—carefully consider the choices that are very similar.

✓ TEACHING TIP FOR THIS SECTION

Tell children that they can more easily solve a probability problem if they circle the element that appears most often. For example, have children circle the ▨ card for the ● problem on page 25. Explain that because there are more of these cards, they are more likely to be chosen from the bag (b).

➡ Answers are on page 40.

Data Analysis and Probability

Concepts: Data Analysis and Probability

Math Concept	page 25	page 26	page 27	page 28	page 29	page 30	page 31	page 32	page 33	page 34	page 35	page 36	page 37	page 38	page 39
Problem Set															
Probability	X	X	X	X	X										
Data Analysis						X	X	X	X	X	X	X	X	X	X
Money				X											
Pictographs						X									
Bar Graphs							X	X							
Measurement									X						
Tables										X	X	X	X	X	
Time											X		X		
Addition														X	X

24 Data Analysis and Probability

You choose one of these cards from a bag without looking.
Which card are you most likely to choose?

ⓐ   ⓑ   ⓒ   ⓓ

EXTEND THE THINKING: Tell why you think you will choose that card.

You choose one of these cards from a bag without looking.
Which card are you most likely to choose?

ⓐ   ⓑ   ⓒ   ⓓ

EXTEND THE THINKING: Tell why you think you will choose that card.

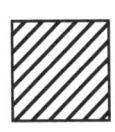

You choose one of these cards from a bag without looking.
Which card are you most likely to choose?

ⓐ   ⓑ   ⓒ   ⓓ

EXTEND THE THINKING: Tell why you think you will choose that card.

Data Analysis and Probability

You choose one of these cards from a bag without looking.
Which card are you most likely to choose?

ⓐ ⓑ ⓒ ⓓ

EXTEND THE THINKING: Tell why you think you will choose that card.

You choose one of these cards from a bag without looking.
Which card are you most likely to choose?

ⓐ ⓑ ⓒ ⓓ

EXTEND THE THINKING: Tell why you think you will choose that card.

You choose one of these cards from a bag without looking.
Which card are you most likely to choose?

ⓐ ⓑ ⓒ ⓓ

EXTEND THE THINKING: Tell why you think you will choose that card.

Data Analysis and Probability

| 4 | 2 | 4 | 4 |

These 4 cards are shuffled and placed facedown on a table. If you flip over 1 card, which card are you most likely to flip over?

ⓐ 7   ⓑ 4   ⓒ 2   ⓓ 9

EXTEND THE THINKING: Tell why you think you will flip over that card.

| 7 | 3 | 3 | 1 |

These 4 cards are shuffled and placed facedown on a table. If you flip over 1 card, which card are you most likely to flip over?

ⓐ 7   ⓑ 3   ⓒ 9   ⓓ 1

EXTEND THE THINKING: Tell why you think you will flip over that card.

| 6 | 2 | 4 | 6 |

These 4 cards are shuffled and placed facedown on a table. If you flip over 1 card, which card are you most likely to flip over?

ⓐ 2   ⓑ 0   ⓒ 4   ⓓ 6

EXTEND THE THINKING: Tell why you think you will flip over that card.

Data Analysis and Probability

You choose one of these coins from a bag without looking. Which coin are you most likely to choose?

ⓐ one cent ⓑ one dime ⓒ five cents ⓓ quarter dollar

EXTEND THE THINKING: Tell why you think you will choose that coin.

You choose one of these coins from a bag without looking. Which coin are you most likely to choose?

ⓐ one cent ⓑ one dime ⓒ five cents ⓓ quarter dollar

EXTEND THE THINKING: Tell why you think you will choose that coin.

You choose one of these coins from a bag without looking. Which coin are you most likely to choose?

ⓐ one cent ⓑ one dime ⓒ quarter dollar ⓓ five cents

EXTEND THE THINKING: Tell why you think you will choose that coin.

These animals are in the barn. If 1 animal leaves the barn, which animal will most likely leave?

ⓐ  ⓑ  ⓒ  ⓓ

EXTEND THE THINKING: Tell why you think that animal is most likely to leave.

These animals are in the barn. If 1 animal leaves the barn, which animal will most likely leave?

ⓐ  ⓑ  ⓒ  ⓓ

EXTEND THE THINKING: Tell why you think that animal is most likely to leave.

These animals are in the barn. If 1 animal leaves the barn, which animal will most likely leave?

ⓐ  ⓑ  ⓒ  ⓓ

EXTEND THE THINKING: Tell why you think that animal is most likely to leave.

Data Analysis and Probability

Favorite Ice-Cream Flavor

Which ice-cream flavor do most of the children like the best?

Flavors	
Chocolate	2 cones
Vanilla	3 cones
Mint Chip	6 cones

ⓐ strawberry   ⓑ chocolate   ⓒ vanilla   ⓓ mint chip

EXTEND THE THINKING: How many more children liked that flavor than chocolate?

Favorite Ice-Cream Flavor

Which ice-cream flavor do 6 children like the best?

Flavors	
Chocolate	2 cones
Vanilla	3 cones
Mint Chip	6 cones

ⓐ strawberry   ⓑ chocolate   ⓒ vanilla   ⓓ mint chip

EXTEND THE THINKING: How many more children liked mint chip than both of the other flavors put together?

Favorite Ice-Cream Flavor

Which ice-cream flavor is the least popular?

Flavors	
Chocolate	2 cones
Vanilla	3 cones
Mint Chip	6 cones

ⓐ strawberry   ⓑ chocolate   ⓒ vanilla   ⓓ mint chip

EXTEND THE THINKING: How many more children liked vanilla than chocolate?

Data Analysis and Probability

Favorite Dessert

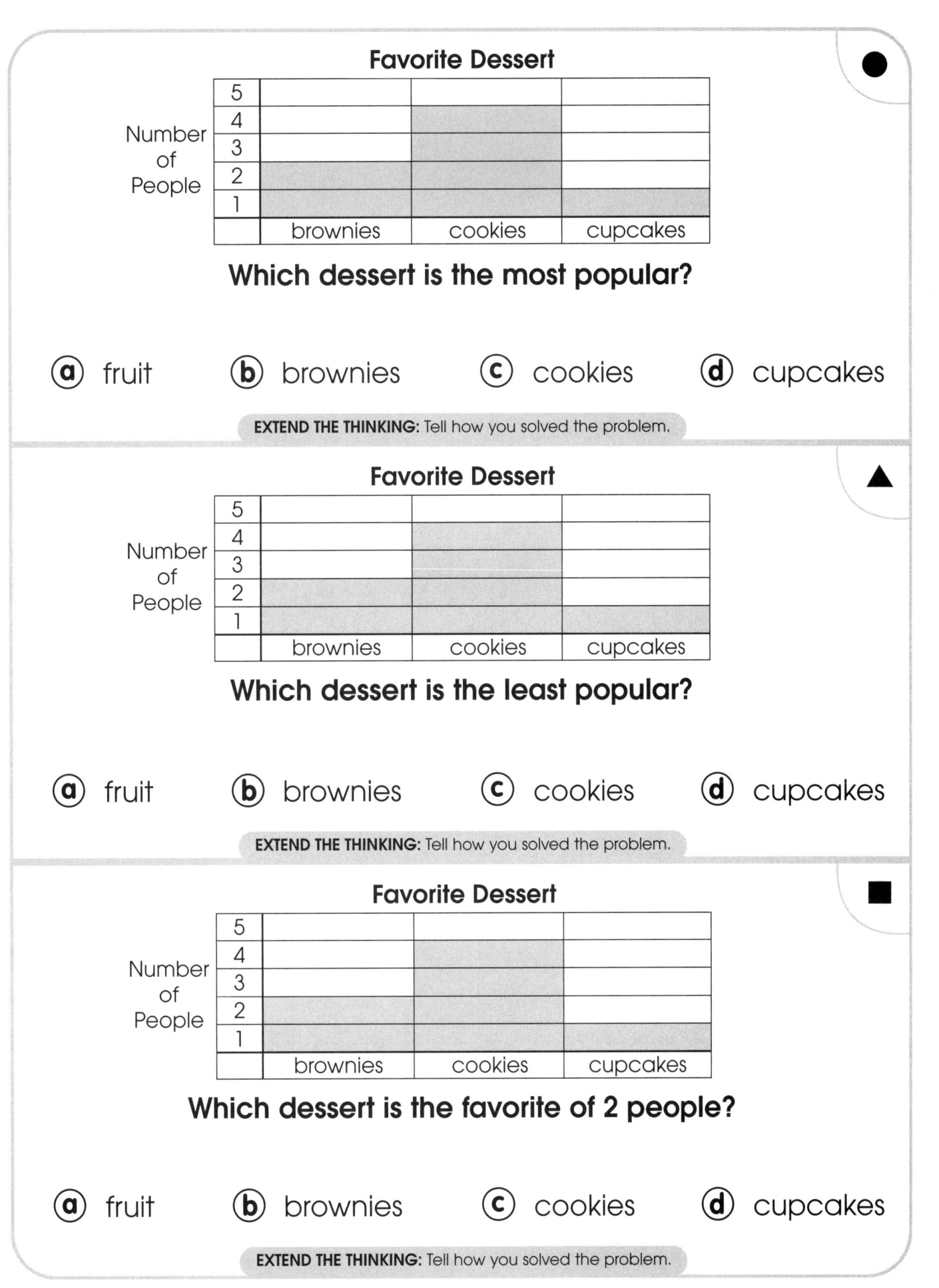

Number of People	brownies	cookies	cupcakes
5			
4		■	
3		■	
2	■	■	
1	■	■	■

Which dessert is the most popular?

ⓐ fruit   ⓑ brownies   ⓒ cookies   ⓓ cupcakes

EXTEND THE THINKING: Tell how you solved the problem.

Favorite Dessert

Number of People	brownies	cookies	cupcakes
5			
4		■	
3		■	
2	■	■	
1	■	■	■

Which dessert is the least popular?

ⓐ fruit   ⓑ brownies   ⓒ cookies   ⓓ cupcakes

EXTEND THE THINKING: Tell how you solved the problem.

Favorite Dessert

Number of People	brownies	cookies	cupcakes
5			
4		■	
3		■	
2	■	■	■
1	■	■	■

Which dessert is the favorite of 2 people?

ⓐ fruit   ⓑ brownies   ⓒ cookies   ⓓ cupcakes

EXTEND THE THINKING: Tell how you solved the problem.

Favorite Sport

Number of People	baseball	soccer	basketball	football
5				
4			■	
3	■		■	
2	■	■	■	
1	■	■	■	■

Which sport is the most popular?

ⓐ volleyball ⓑ basketball ⓒ soccer ⓓ football

EXTEND THE THINKING: Tell how you solved the problem.

Favorite Sport

Number of People	baseball	soccer	basketball	football
5				
4			■	
3	■		■	
2	■		■	
1	■	■	■	■

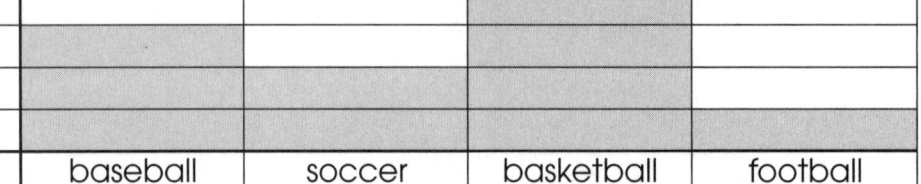

Which sport is the least popular?

ⓐ baseball ⓑ soccer ⓒ basketball ⓓ football

EXTEND THE THINKING: Tell how you solved the problem.

Favorite Sport

Number of People	baseball	soccer	basketball	football
5				
4			■	
3	■		■	
2	■	■	■	
1	■	■	■	■

Which sport is more popular than soccer but less popular than basketball?

ⓐ baseball ⓑ soccer ⓒ basketball ⓓ football

EXTEND THE THINKING: Tell how you solved the problem.

32 Data Analysis and Probability

How much sugar do you need to make these cookies?

recipe
2 cups flour
½ cup sugar
1 cup chocolate chips

(a) 1 tablespoon   (b) 2 cups   (c) ½ cup   (d) 1 cup

EXTEND THE THINKING: How much sugar do you need to make twice as many cookies?

You need the most of which ingredient?

recipe
2 cups flour
1 cup sugar
1 cup chocolate chips

(a) flour   (b) sugar   (c) chocolate chips   (d) water

EXTEND THE THINKING: How much more of that ingredient than chocolate chips do you need?

You need the least of which ingredient?

recipe
2 cups flour
½ cup sugar
1 cup chocolate chips

(a) water   (b) sugar   (c) chocolate chips   (d) flour

EXTEND THE THINKING: How much of that ingredient do you need to make half as many cookies?

Data Analysis and Probability 33

Today's Score	
Jets	9
Panthers	15

Who is winning the game?

ⓐ Lions   ⓑ Rockets   ⓒ Jets   ⓓ Panthers

EXTEND THE THINKING: How far ahead is the winning team?

Today's Score	
Jets	27
Panthers	15

Who is winning the game?

ⓐ Jets   ⓑ Lions   ⓒ Rockets   ⓓ Panthers

EXTEND THE THINKING: How far ahead is the winning team?

Today's Score	
Jets	64
Panthers	46

Who is winning the game?

ⓐ Lions   ⓑ Rockets   ⓒ Jets   ⓓ Panthers

EXTEND THE THINKING: How far ahead is the winning team?

Lunch Menu

Mon.	Tue.	Wed.	Thurs.	Fri.
hamburgers	hot dogs	tacos	spaghetti	pizza

What is for lunch on Wednesday?

(a) tacos (b) hot dogs (c) sandwiches (d) pizza

EXTEND THE THINKING: What is for lunch 2 days later?

Lunch Menu

Mon.	Tue.	Wed.	Thurs.	Fri.
hamburgers	hot dogs	tacos	spaghetti	pizza

Hamburgers are for lunch on Monday. What is for lunch 3 days later?

(a) spaghetti (b) pizza (c) tacos (d) hot dogs

EXTEND THE THINKING: What is for lunch 4 days after Monday?

Lunch Menu

Mon.	Tue.	Wed.	Thurs.	Fri.
hamburgers	hot dogs	tacos	spaghetti	pizza

What is for lunch the day after tacos?

(a) tacos (b) hot dogs (c) spaghetti (d) pizza

EXTEND THE THINKING: What is for lunch the day before Tuesday?

Data Analysis and Probability

Week's Weather

Mon.	Tue.	Wed.	Thurs.	Fri.
sunny	rainy cloud	rainy cloud	snowy cloud	rainy cloud

How was the weather on Wednesday?

ⓐ rainy ⓑ rainy cloud ⓒ sunny ⓓ snowy cloud

EXTEND THE THINKING: Which other day had that type of weather that week?

Week's Weather

Mon.	Tue.	Wed.	Thurs.	Fri.
sunny	rainy cloud	rainy cloud	snowy cloud	rainy cloud

How was the weather on Thursday?

ⓐ sunny ⓑ rainy cloud ⓒ rainy ⓓ snowy cloud

EXTEND THE THINKING: What was the weather like 2 days earlier?

Week's Weather

Mon.	Tue.	Wed.	Thurs.	Fri.
sunny	rainy cloud	rainy cloud	rainy cloud	rainy cloud

Most of the days had what kind of weather?

ⓐ rainy ⓑ rainy cloud ⓒ sunny ⓓ snowy cloud

EXTEND THE THINKING: How many sunny days were there?

36 Data Analysis and Probability

TV Schedule

	7:00
Channel 3	Wild Animals
Channel 6	On the Go!
Channel 8	Zap!

What show is on channel 3 at 7:00?

ⓐ Monkey Talk   ⓑ The Silly Billies   ⓒ Zap!   ⓓ Wild Animals

EXTEND THE THINKING: Name another show that is on at the same time.

TV Schedule

	7:00	7:30
Channel 3	Wild Animals	Catch It!
Channel 6	On the Go!	Plant Life
Channel 8	Zap!	The Silly Billies

What show is on channel 6 at 7:30?

ⓐ Catch It!   ⓑ The Silly Billies   ⓒ On the Go!   ⓓ Plant Life

EXTEND THE THINKING: Which other shows could you watch at that time? Tell why.

TV Schedule

	7:00	7:30
Channel 3	Wild Animals	Catch It!
Channel 6	On the Go!	Plant Life
Channel 8	Zap!	The Silly Billies

What show comes on after On the Go! on the same channel?

ⓐ Plant Life   ⓑ The Silly Billies   ⓒ Zap!   ⓓ Wild Animals

EXTEND THE THINKING: If the shows are all 30 minutes long, at what time will the next show start?

Carnival Prize Chart

5 points	= pencil
10 points	= pinball game
15 points	= teddy bear
20 points	= piggy bank

You scored 15 points. Which prize did you win?

ⓐ pencil   **ⓑ** pinball game   **ⓒ** teddy bear   **ⓓ** piggy bank

EXTEND THE THINKING: Which prize could you get if you scored 5 more points?

Carnival Prize Chart

5 points	= pencil
10 points	= pinball game
15 points	= teddy bear
20 points	= piggy bank

You scored 20 points. Which of these prizes did you win?

ⓐ 2 pencils   **ⓑ** 1 pinball game   **ⓒ** 2 piggy banks   **ⓓ** 2 pinball games

EXTEND THE THINKING: Which additional prize could you get if you scored 5 more points?

Carnival Prize Chart

5 points	= pencil
10 points	= pinball game
15 points	= teddy bear
20 points	= piggy bank

You scored 25 points. Which of these groups of prizes did you win?

ⓐ piggy bank and teddy bear   **ⓑ** pinball game and piggy bank   **ⓒ** 2 teddy bears   **ⓓ** piggy bank and pencil

EXTEND THE THINKING: Which prize could you get if you scored 10 more points?

5¢ 10¢ 25¢ 20¢

Which item is the least expensive?

ⓐ ⓑ ⓒ ⓓ

EXTEND THE THINKING: Which coins could you use to pay for the item?

5¢ 10¢ 25¢ 20¢

Which item is the most expensive?

ⓐ ⓑ ⓒ ⓓ

EXTEND THE THINKING: Which coins could you use to pay for the item?

5¢ 10¢ 25¢ 20¢

Which item could you buy with 10¢?

ⓐ ⓑ ⓒ ⓓ

EXTEND THE THINKING: Which coins could you use to pay for the item?

Data Analysis and Probability

Section Answers
Data Analysis and Probability

Correct answers are shaded.

	page 25	page 26	page 27	page 28	page 29
○	ⓐ **ⓑ** ⓒ ⓓ	**ⓐ** ⓑ ⓒ ⓓ	ⓐ **ⓑ** ⓒ ⓓ	ⓐ ⓑ **ⓒ** ⓓ	**ⓐ** ⓑ ⓒ ⓓ
△	ⓐ **ⓑ** ⓒ ⓓ	ⓐ ⓑ **ⓒ** ⓓ	ⓐ **ⓑ** ⓒ ⓓ	ⓐ ⓑ **ⓒ** ⓓ	ⓐ ⓑ ⓒ **ⓓ**
□	ⓐ ⓑ **ⓒ** ⓓ	**ⓐ** ⓑ ⓒ ⓓ	ⓐ ⓑ ⓒ **ⓓ**	ⓐ ⓑ ⓒ **ⓓ**	ⓐ **ⓑ** ⓒ ⓓ

	page 30	page 31	page 32	page 33	page 34
○	ⓐ ⓑ ⓒ **ⓓ**	ⓐ ⓑ **ⓒ** ⓓ	ⓐ **ⓑ** ⓒ ⓓ	ⓐ ⓑ **ⓒ** ⓓ	ⓐ ⓑ ⓒ **ⓓ**
△	ⓐ ⓑ ⓒ **ⓓ**	ⓐ ⓑ ⓒ **ⓓ**	ⓐ ⓑ ⓒ **ⓓ**	**ⓐ** ⓑ ⓒ ⓓ	**ⓐ** ⓑ ⓒ ⓓ
□	ⓐ **ⓑ** ⓒ ⓓ	ⓐ **ⓑ** ⓒ ⓓ	**ⓐ** ⓑ ⓒ ⓓ	ⓐ **ⓑ** ⓒ ⓓ	ⓐ ⓑ **ⓒ** ⓓ

	page 35	page 36	page 37	page 38	page 39
○	**ⓐ** ⓑ ⓒ ⓓ	ⓐ **ⓑ** ⓒ ⓓ	ⓐ ⓑ ⓒ **ⓓ**	ⓐ ⓑ **ⓒ** ⓓ	ⓐ ⓑ ⓒ **ⓓ**
△	**ⓐ** ⓑ ⓒ ⓓ	ⓐ ⓑ ⓒ **ⓓ**	ⓐ ⓑ ⓒ **ⓓ**	ⓐ ⓑ ⓒ **ⓓ**	ⓐ ⓑ **ⓒ** ⓓ
□	ⓐ ⓑ **ⓒ** ⓓ	ⓐ **ⓑ** ⓒ ⓓ	**ⓐ** ⓑ ⓒ ⓓ	ⓐ ⓑ ⓒ **ⓓ**	ⓐ **ⓑ** ⓒ ⓓ

Geometry and Spatial Relationships

The *Level A* Geometry and Spatial Relationships standards require children to

- identify shapes and solids
- compare attributes of a shape such as the number of sides, angles, or corners
- identify real-life objects that share the same attributes as a given geometric shape
- understand the concept of symmetry: "same on both sides"
- make a design symmetrical by creating a mirrored image
- complete spatial design tasks

Making Solids

Make out of pipe cleaners 3-D shapes that represent solids. Have children count the number of sides and corners on the different solids. Then, invite children to make each solid out of toothpicks and mini-marshmallows.

Geoboard Symmetry

Arrange the class into pairs. Give each pair a geoboard and some rubber bands. Invite the first partner to use the rubber bands to create symmetrical designs on the pegs of the geoboard. Have the other partner create on the same geoboard the mirrored images of the designs.

✏️ TEST-TAKING TIPS
FOR CHILDREN

✔ Avoid selecting answers that are unfamiliar or that you do not understand.

✔ Answer those questions you know first; leave challenging ones for later.

✔ Don't change your answers without good reason.

✓ TEACHING TIP
FOR THIS SECTION

Tell children that they can more easily solve a geometry problem if they number the sides of each shape. For example, have children number each side of each shape in the ■ problem on page 50. Explain that the triangle has three sides, which is less than the hexagon (six sides) or square (four sides) *(d)*.

→ Answers are on page 58.

Concepts: Geometry and Spatial Relationships

Math Concept	page 43	page 44	page 45	page 46	page 47	page 48	page 49	page 50	page 51	page 52	page 53	page 54	page 55	page 56	page 57
Symmetry	X	X													
Shapes	X	X	X	X	X	X	X	X	X			X	X	X	X
Solids	X	X	X							X	X				
Spatial Relationships												X	X		
Open/Closed Figures															X
Addition												X	X	X	

42 *Geometry and Spatial Relationships*

Which object is the same shape as 🗲 ?

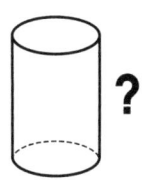

ⓐ ⓑ ⓒ ⓓ

EXTEND THE THINKING: What is the name of that shape?

Which object is the same shape as 🗲 ?

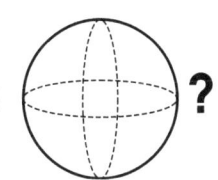

ⓐ ⓑ ⓒ ⓓ

EXTEND THE THINKING: What is the name of that shape?

Which object is the same shape as 🗲 ?

ⓐ ⓑ ⓒ ⓓ

EXTEND THE THINKING: What is the name of that shape?

Geometry and Spatial Relationships

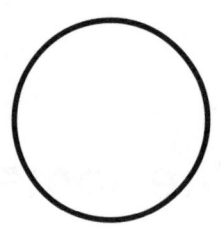

What is the name of this shape?

ⓐ circle　　ⓑ square　　ⓒ triangle　　ⓓ rectangle

EXTEND THE THINKING: What do we have in our world that comes in that shape?

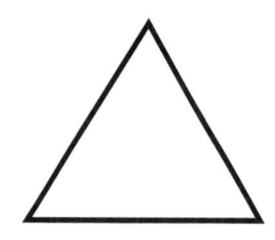

What is the name of this shape?

ⓐ circle　　ⓑ square　　ⓒ triangle　　ⓓ rectangle

EXTEND THE THINKING: What do we have in our world that comes in that shape?

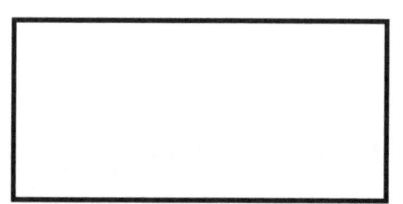

What is the name of this shape?

ⓐ circle　　ⓑ square　　ⓒ triangle　　ⓓ rectangle

EXTEND THE THINKING: What do we have in our world that comes in that shape?

46 *Geometry and Spatial Relationships*

What is the name of this shape?

ⓐ circle　　ⓑ oval　　ⓒ triangle　　ⓓ rectangle

EXTEND THE THINKING: What do we have in our world that comes in that shape?

What is the name of this shape?

ⓐ circle　　ⓑ square　　ⓒ triangle　　ⓓ rectangle

EXTEND THE THINKING: What do we have in our world that comes in that shape?

What is the name of this shape?

ⓐ hexagon　　ⓑ square　　ⓒ triangle　　ⓓ rectangle

EXTEND THE THINKING: What do we have in our world that comes in that shape?

Geometry and Spatial Relationships

[square]

How many sides are on this shape?

ⓐ 1   ⓑ 2   ⓒ 4   ⓓ 3

EXTEND THE THINKING: What do we have in our world that comes in that shape?

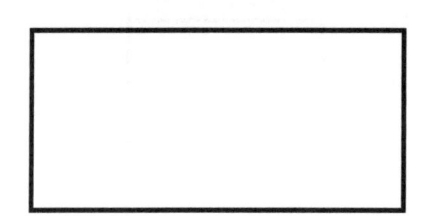

[rectangle]

How many sides are on this shape?

ⓐ 1   ⓑ 2   ⓒ 4   ⓓ 3

EXTEND THE THINKING: What do we have in our world that comes in that shape?

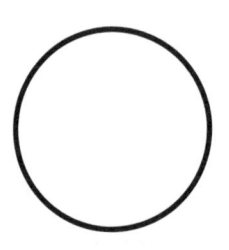

[circle]

How many sides are on this shape?

ⓐ 4   ⓑ 0   ⓒ 1   ⓓ 3

EXTEND THE THINKING: What do we have in our world that comes in that shape?

48   Geometry and Spatial Relationships

How many corners are on this shape?

ⓐ 3 ⓑ 2 ⓒ 1 ⓓ 4

EXTEND THE THINKING: What do we have in our world that comes in that shape?

How many corners are on this shape?

ⓐ 4 ⓑ 2 ⓒ 1 ⓓ 3

EXTEND THE THINKING: What do we have in our world that comes in that shape?

How many corners are on this shape?

ⓐ 6 ⓑ 2 ⓒ 8 ⓓ 5

EXTEND THE THINKING: What do we have in our world that comes in that shape?

Geometry and Spatial Relationships **49**

Which shape has 4 corners?

ⓐ rectangle   ⓑ square   ⓒ triangle   ⓓ hexagon

EXTEND THE THINKING: What do we have in our world that comes in that shape?

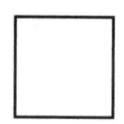

Which shape has the greatest number of sides?

ⓐ rectangle   ⓑ square   ⓒ circle   ⓓ hexagon

EXTEND THE THINKING: What do we have in our world that comes in that shape?

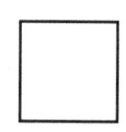

Which shape has the least number of sides?

ⓐ rectangle   ⓑ square   ⓒ hexagon   ⓓ triangle

EXTEND THE THINKING: What do we have in our world that comes in that shape?

50   Geometry and Spatial Relationships

Which shape has the longest sides?

ⓐ rectangle ⓑ square ⓒ circle ⓓ triangle

EXTEND THE THINKING: What do we have in our world that comes in that shape?

Which shape has the least number of sides?

ⓐ rectangle ⓑ square ⓒ circle ⓓ triangle

EXTEND THE THINKING: What do we have in our world that comes in that shape?

Which shape has 4 sides of equal length?

ⓐ rectangle ⓑ square ⓒ circle ⓓ triangle

EXTEND THE THINKING: What do we have in our world that comes in that shape?

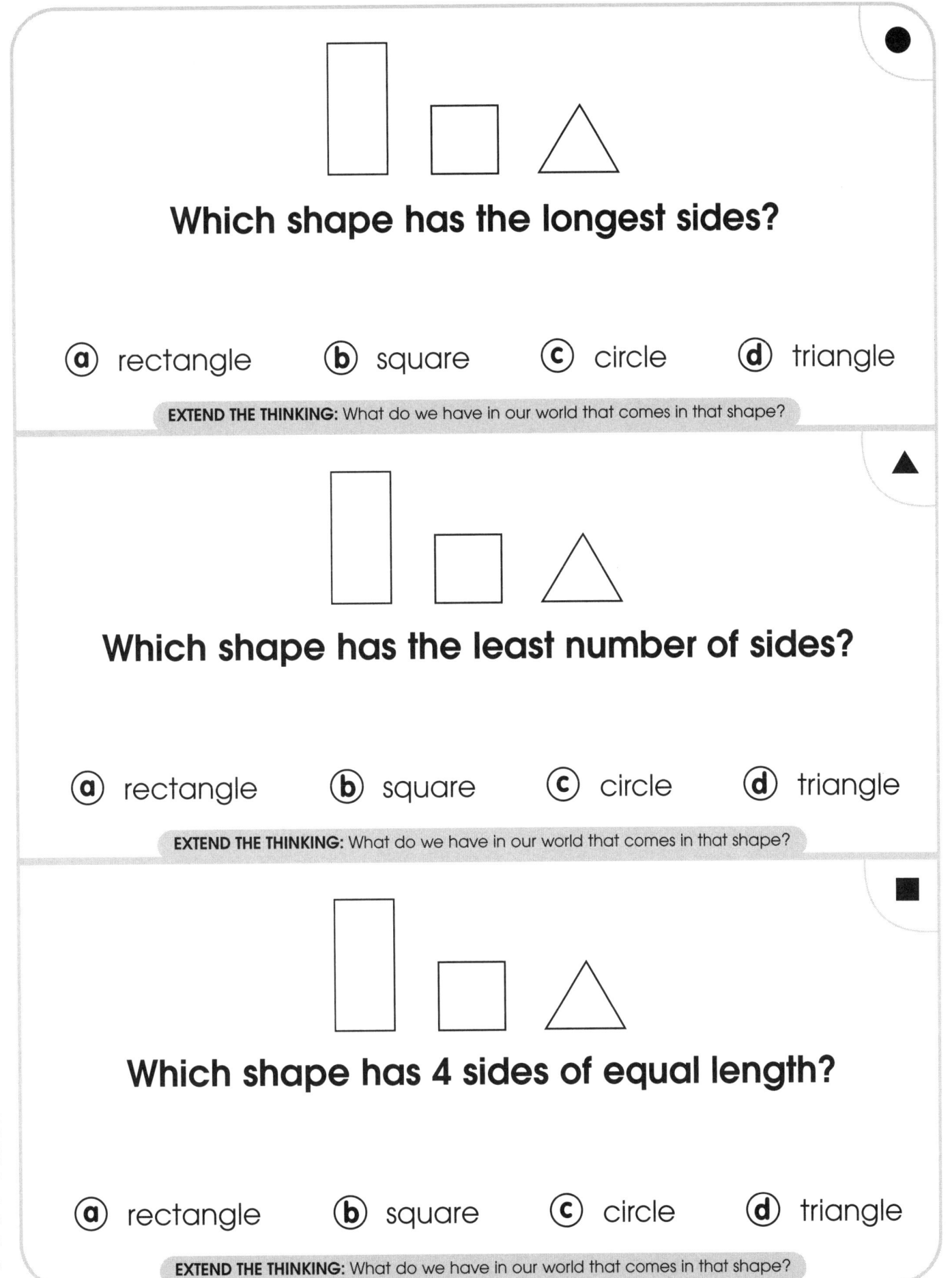

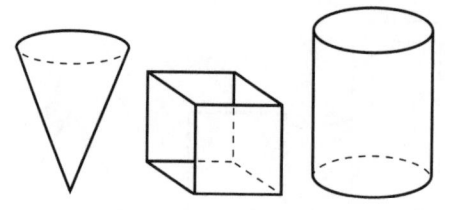

What is the name of the tallest solid?

ⓐ cube　　ⓑ cylinder　　ⓒ square　　ⓓ triangle

EXTEND THE THINKING: What do we have in our world that comes in that shape?

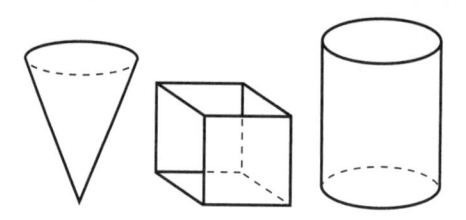

What is the name of the shortest solid?

ⓐ cube　　ⓑ cone　　ⓒ rectangular prism　　ⓓ cylinder

EXTEND THE THINKING: What do we have in our world that comes in that shape?

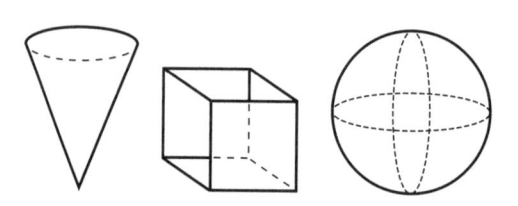

What is the name of the widest solid?

ⓐ cube　　ⓑ cone　　ⓒ sphere　　ⓓ cylinder

EXTEND THE THINKING: What do we have in our world that comes in that shape?

Geometry and Spatial Relationships

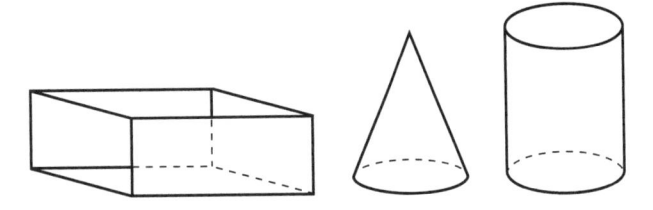

Which solid has 6 faces?

ⓐ square   ⓑ cylinder   ⓒ rectangular prism   ⓓ cone

EXTEND THE THINKING: What do we have in our world that comes in that shape?

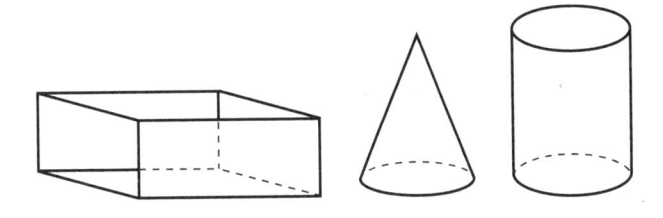

Which solid has 2 circular faces?

ⓐ cube   ⓑ cone   ⓒ cylinder   ⓓ rectangular prism

EXTEND THE THINKING: What do we have in our world that comes in that shape?

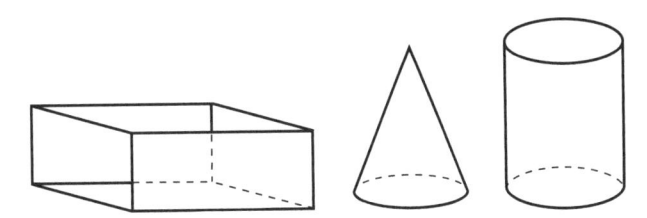

Which solid has less than 3 faces?

ⓐ cube   ⓑ cone   ⓒ rectangular prism   ⓓ cylinder

EXTEND THE THINKING: What do we have in our world that comes in that shape?

Geometry and Spatial Relationships 53

6 steps 6 steps

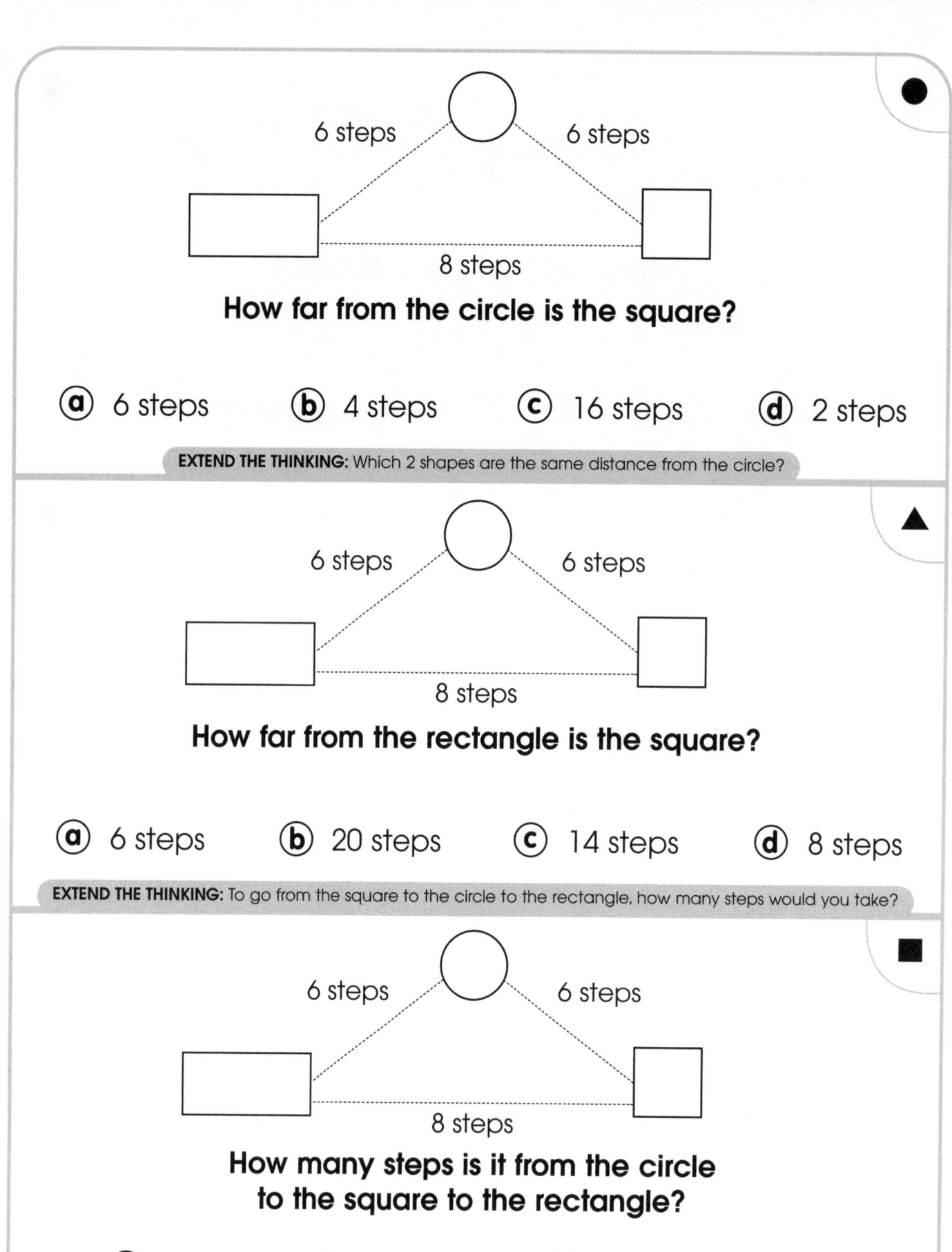

8 steps

How far from the circle is the square?

ⓐ 6 steps   ⓑ 4 steps   ⓒ 16 steps   ⓓ 2 steps

EXTEND THE THINKING: Which 2 shapes are the same distance from the circle?

6 steps 6 steps

8 steps

How far from the rectangle is the square?

ⓐ 6 steps   ⓑ 20 steps   ⓒ 14 steps   ⓓ 8 steps

EXTEND THE THINKING: To go from the square to the circle to the rectangle, how many steps would you take?

6 steps 6 steps

8 steps

How many steps is it from the circle to the square to the rectangle?

ⓐ 6   ⓑ 12   ⓒ 14   ⓓ 8

EXTEND THE THINKING: How many steps is it all the way around?

54 *Geometry and Spatial Relationships*

What is the shortest path from the circle to the triangle?

ⓐ 8 steps   ⓑ 5 steps   ⓒ 10 steps   ⓓ 13 steps

EXTEND THE THINKING: Which 2 shapes are the same distance from the triangle?

What is the shortest path from the circle to the square?

ⓐ 8 steps   ⓑ 5 steps   ⓒ 16 steps   ⓓ 2 steps

EXTEND THE THINKING: Which shape is closest to the circle?

How many steps is it from the triangle to the square to the circle?

ⓐ 8   ⓑ 5   ⓒ 13   ⓓ 10

EXTEND THE THINKING: How many steps is it all the way around?

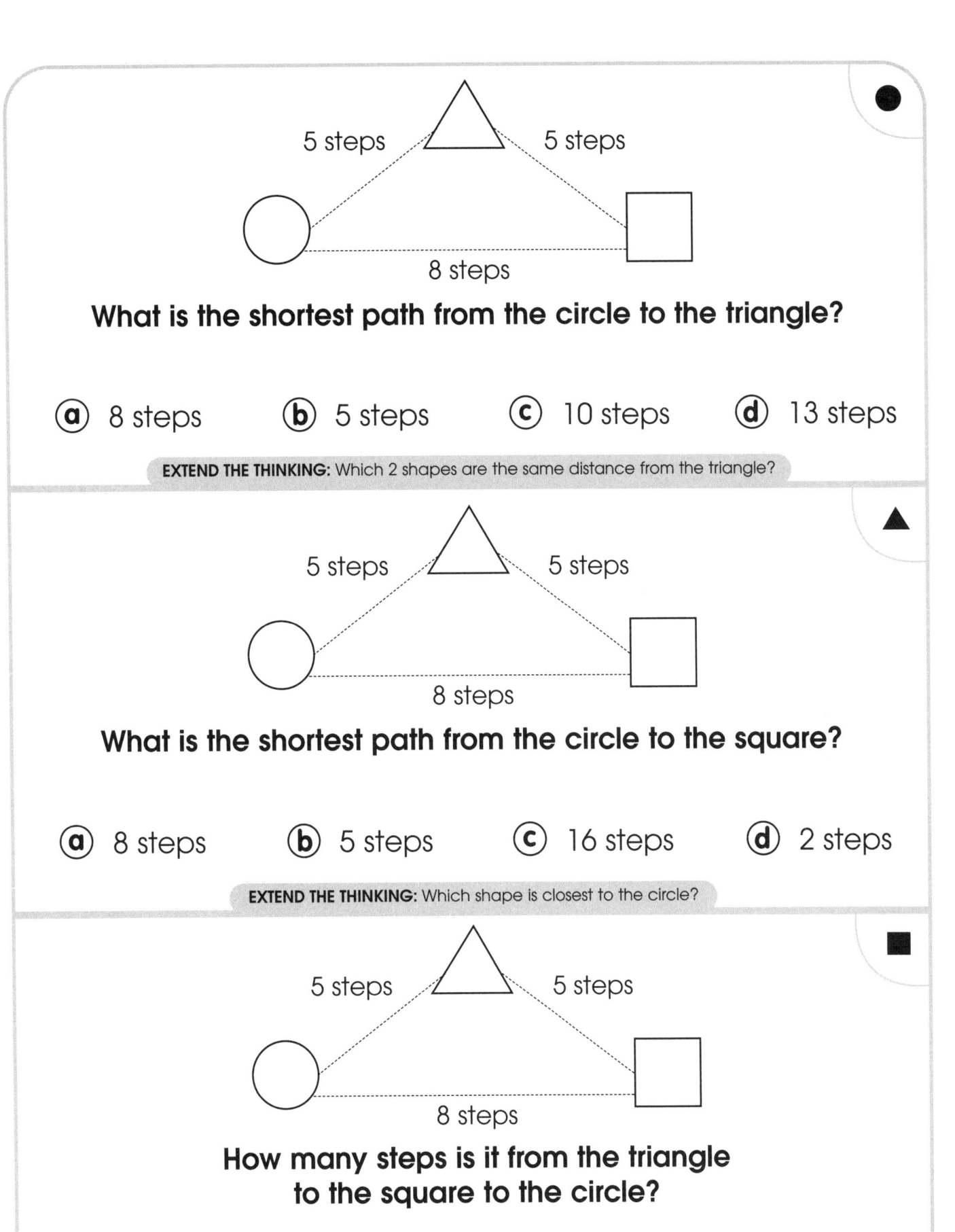

Geometry and Spatial Relationships 55

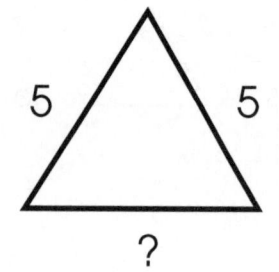

5 △ 5
?

If all sides are equal length, how long is the unlabeled side?

ⓐ 10   ⓑ 2   ⓒ 15   ⓓ 5

EXTEND THE THINKING: What is the name of that shape?

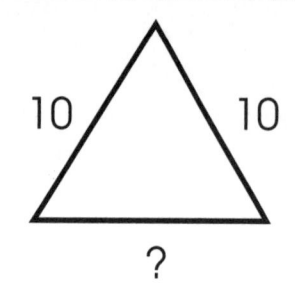

---

10 △ 10
?

If all sides are equal length, how long is the unlabeled side?

ⓐ 10   ⓑ 2   ⓒ 15   ⓓ 5

EXTEND THE THINKING: Tell how you solved the problem.

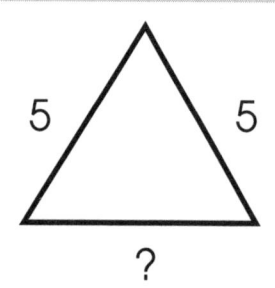

---

5 △ 5
?

If all sides are equal length, what is the total length of all the sides?

ⓐ 10   ⓑ 5   ⓒ 15   ⓓ 50

EXTEND THE THINKING: Tell how you solved the problem.

Geometry and Spatial Relationships

Which is the open figure?

(a) ▢ (b) △ (c) ○ (d) ⊔

EXTEND THE THINKING: Draw another open figure.

Which is the closed figure?

(a) ▢ (b) ⊓ (c) ⊃ (d) ⎵

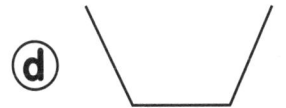

EXTEND THE THINKING: Draw another closed figure.

C S D F

Which is the closed figure?

(a) S (b) D (c) C (d) F

EXTEND THE THINKING: Write another letter that is a closed figure.

Section Answers
Geometry and Spatial Relationships

Correct answers are shaded.

	page 43	page 44	page 45	page 46	page 47
○	**a** b c d	**a** b c d	a b **c** d	**a** b c d	a **b** c d
△	a b **c** d	a **b** c d	**a** b c d	a b **c** d	a **b** c d
□	a **b** c d	**a** b c d	a **b** c d	a b c **d**	**a** b c d

	page 48	page 49	page 50	page 51	page 52
○	a b **c** d	a b c **d**	a **b** c d	**a** b c d	a **b** c d
△	a b **c** d	**a** b c d	a b c **d**	a b c **d**	**a** b c d
□	a **b** c d	**a** b c d	a b c **d**	a **b** c d	a b **c** d

	page 53	page 54	page 55	page 56	page 57
○	a b **c** d	**a** b c d	a **b** c d	a b c **d**	a b c **d**
△	a b **c** d	a b c **d**	**a** b c d	**a** b c d	**a** b c d
□	a **b** c d	a b c **d**	**a** b c d	a b **c** d	a **b** c d

58 Geometry and Spatial Relationships

Logic and Critical Thinking

The *Level A* Logic and Critical Thinking standards require children to

- compare and contrast numbers
- identify odd/even and greater than/less than
- apply the concepts of ordinal numbers
- apply a variety of strategies to solve problems and identify mystery numbers

Manipulative Logic

Give each child a set of four different-colored manipulatives (e.g., plastic bears or spiders). Provide clues to help children arrange the manipulatives in the correct order. Begin with simple clues, and progress as the children become proficient. For example, say *The red bear is first. The blue bear is last. The yellow bear is next to the red bear. The green bear is before the blue bear. What do they look like in a row?*

Kinesthetic Logic

Shuffle number cards, and give one to each child. For example, if you have 20 children, pass out cards numbered from 1 to 20. Have children arrange themselves in order. Give clues that help children apply the concepts of number sequence and greater than/less than to discover a "Mystery Number." For example, say *The number is greater than 5.* Have children with cards from 1 to 5 sit down. Say *The number is less than 15.* Have children with cards from 15 to 20 sit down. Say *The number is an odd number.* Have children with cards 6, 8, 10, 12, and 14 sit down. Say *The number is less than 9 and greater than 5.* The child holding the 7 card has the mystery number.

TEST-TAKING TIPS
FOR CHILDREN

✔ Get lots of sleep the night before a test.

✔ Avoid rushing—lay out the things you need for school the night before the test.

TEACHING TIP
FOR THIS SECTION

Tell children that they can sometimes more easily solve a logic problem by drawing a picture. Have them cover the answers to the ● problem on page 61 and draw a picture that illustrates the problem. Then, have them uncover the answers and match their drawing to the correct answer (*d*).

→ Answers are on page 76.

Concepts: Logic and Critical Thinking

Math Concept	page 61	page 62	page 63	page 64	page 65	page 66	page 67	page 68	page 69	page 70	page 71	page 72	page 73	page 74	page 75
Logic	X	X	X	X	X	X									
Critical Thinking							X	X	X	X	X	X	X	X	X
Ordinal Numbers	X	X													
Shapes		X													
Subtraction									X	X					
Odd/Even Numbers											X	X			
Addition							X	X				X	X	X	X
Pictographs													X	X	X

Problem Set

60 Logic and Critical Thinking

**The frog is first,
the cat is second,
and the rabbit is third.
What do they look
like in a row?**

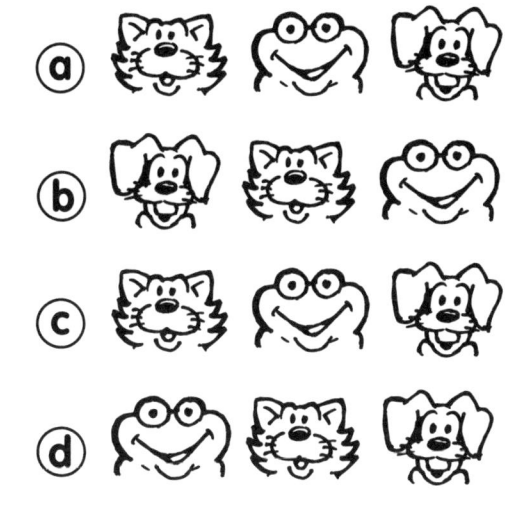

ⓐ cat frog dog
ⓑ dog cat frog
ⓒ cat frog dog
ⓓ frog cat dog

EXTEND THE THINKING: Tell how you solved the problem.

**The frog is second,
the cat is first,
and the rabbit is third.
What do they look
like in a row?**

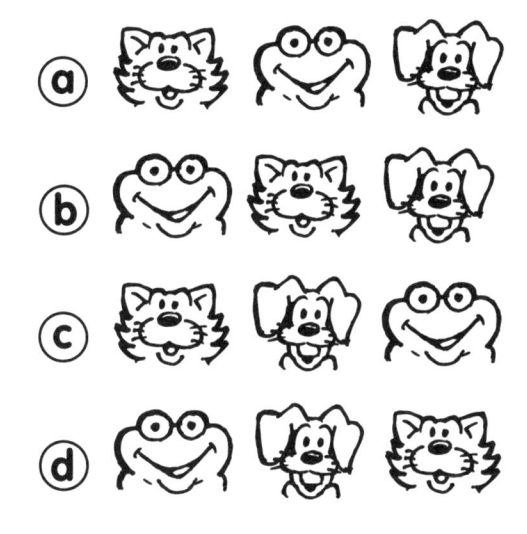

ⓐ cat frog dog
ⓑ frog cat dog
ⓒ cat dog frog
ⓓ frog dog cat

EXTEND THE THINKING: Tell how you solved the problem.

**The frog is third,
the cat is first,
and the rabbit is second.
What do they look
like in a row?**

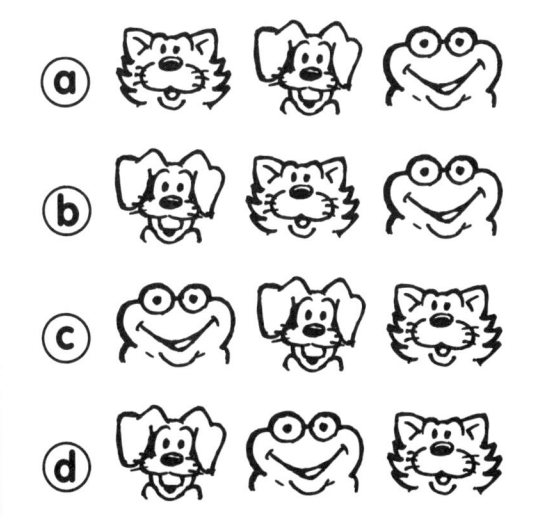

ⓐ cat dog frog
ⓑ dog cat frog
ⓒ frog dog cat
ⓓ dog frog cat

EXTEND THE THINKING: Tell how you solved the problem.

Logic and Critical Thinking

**The square is first,
the circle is second,
and the triangle is third.
What do they look
like in a row?**

ⓐ ▢ ○ △

ⓑ ▢ △ ○

ⓒ ○ ▢ △

ⓓ △ ○ ▢

EXTEND THE THINKING: Tell how you solved the problem.

**The square is second,
the circle is first,
and the triangle is third.
What do they look
like in a row?**

ⓐ ○ ▢ △

ⓑ ○ △ ▢

ⓒ ▢ ○ △

ⓓ △ ▢ ○

EXTEND THE THINKING: Tell how you solved the problem.

**The square is third,
the circle is first,
and the triangle is second.
What do they look
like in a row?**

ⓐ △ ○ ▢

ⓑ △ ▢ ○

ⓒ ○ △ ▢

ⓓ ▢ ○ △

EXTEND THE THINKING: Tell how you solved the problem.

62 Logic and Critical Thinking

**The mystery number is greater than 2 but less than 4.
What is the number?**

(a) 5   (b) 3   (c) 6   (d) none of these choices

EXTEND THE THINKING: Which number is 4 greater than the mystery number?

**The mystery number is greater than 13 but less than 15.
What is the number?**

(a) 14   (b) 10   (c) 12   (d) none of these choices

EXTEND THE THINKING: Which number is 8 greater than the mystery number?

**The mystery number is greater than 10 but less than 17.
What could the number be?**

(a) 15   (b) 10   (c) 19   (d) none of these choices

EXTEND THE THINKING: What are all the possible mystery numbers for this problem?

Logic and Critical Thinking

The mystery number is greater than 5 but less than 7.
What is the number?

(a) 5   (b) 7   (c) 6   (d) none of these choices

EXTEND THE THINKING: Which number is 6 greater than the mystery number?

The mystery number is greater than 10 but less than 12.
What is the number?

(a) 11   (b) 10   (c) 12   (d) none of these choices

EXTEND THE THINKING: Which number is 4 less than the mystery number?

The mystery number is greater than 10 but less than 15.
What could the number be?

(a) 18   (b) 10   (c) 15   (d) none of these choices

EXTEND THE THINKING: What are all the possible mystery numbers for this problem?

64 Logic and Critical Thinking

The mystery number is greater than 6 but less than 8.
What is the number?

(a) 5   (b) 7   (c) 6   (d) none of these choices

EXTEND THE THINKING: Which number is 4 less than the mystery number?

The mystery number is greater than 12 but less than 14.
What is the number?

(a) 10   (b) 13   (c) 12   (d) none of these choices

EXTEND THE THINKING: Which number is 7 greater than the mystery number?

The mystery number is greater than 15 but less than 19.
What could the number be?

(a) 18   (b) 14   (c) 20   (d) none of these choices

EXTEND THE THINKING: What are all the possible mystery numbers for this problem?

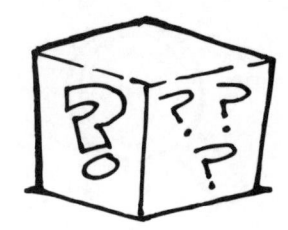

The mystery number is greater than 9 but less than 11.
What is the number?

ⓐ 9   **ⓑ** 7   **ⓒ** 6   **ⓓ** none of these choices

EXTEND THE THINKING: Which number is 5 less than the mystery number?

The mystery number is greater than 16 but less than 18.
What is the number?

ⓐ 19   **ⓑ** 17   **ⓒ** 12   **ⓓ** none of these choices

EXTEND THE THINKING: Which number is 11 less than the mystery number?

The mystery number is greater than 19 but less than 23.
What could the number be?

ⓐ 21   **ⓑ** 19   **ⓒ** 24   **ⓓ** none of these choices

EXTEND THE THINKING: What are all the possible mystery numbers for this problem?

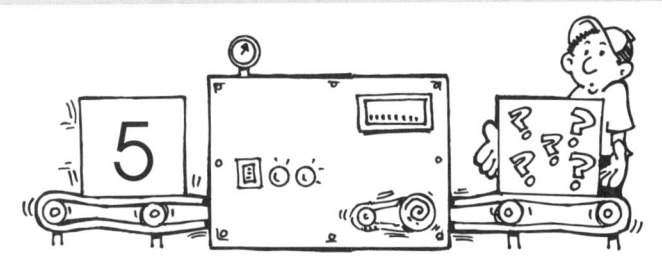

The Magic Number Machine adds 5 to every number that goes in. If 5 goes in, which number comes out?

(a) 5   (b) 10   (c) 15   (d) none of these choices

EXTEND THE THINKING: Write a number sentence that shows what the machine did.

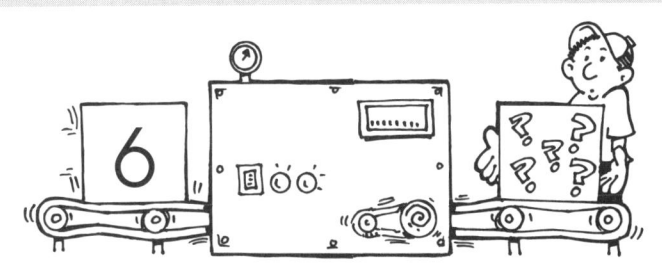

The Magic Number Machine adds 5 to every number that goes in. If 6 goes in, which number comes out?

(a) 56   (b) 10   (c) 11   (d) none of these choices

EXTEND THE THINKING: Write a number sentence that shows what the machine did.

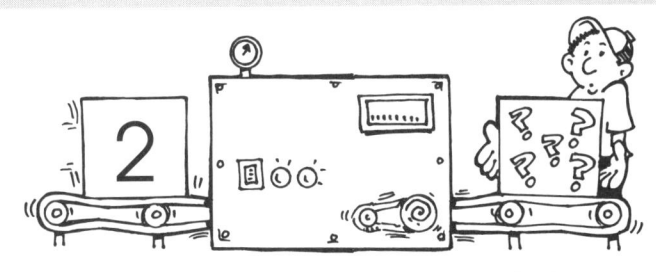

The Magic Number Machine adds 12 to every number that goes in. If 2 goes in, which number comes out?

(a) 19   (b) 14   (c) 21   (d) none of these choices

EXTEND THE THINKING: Write a number sentence that shows what the machine did.

Logic and Critical Thinking

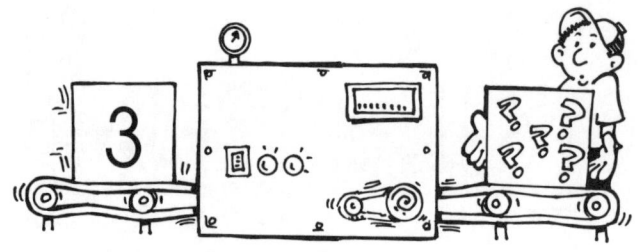

The Magic Number Machine adds 2 to every number that goes in. If 3 goes in, which number comes out?

ⓐ 5   ⓑ 4   ⓒ 1   ⓓ none of these choices

EXTEND THE THINKING: Write a number sentence that shows what the machine did.

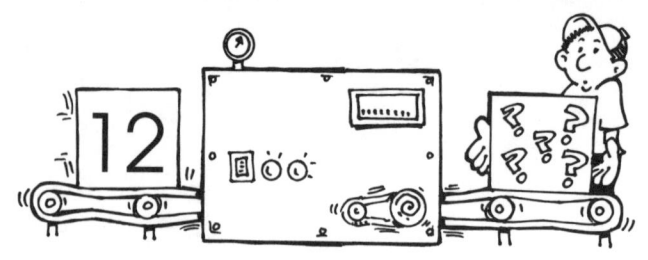

The Magic Number Machine adds 2 to every number that goes in. If 12 goes in, which number comes out?

ⓐ 10   ⓑ 13   ⓒ 16   ⓓ none of these choices

EXTEND THE THINKING: Write a number sentence that shows what the machine did.

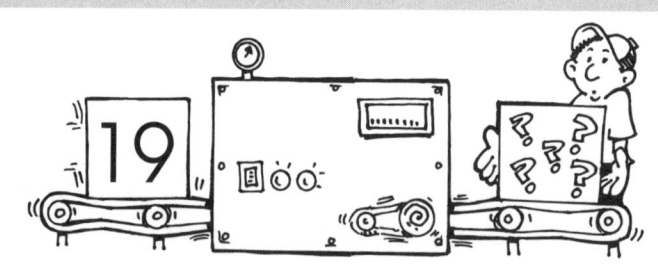

The Magic Number Machine adds 2 to every number that goes in. If 19 goes in, which number comes out?

ⓐ 20   ⓑ 22   ⓒ 21   ⓓ none of these choices

EXTEND THE THINKING: Write a number sentence that shows what the machine did.

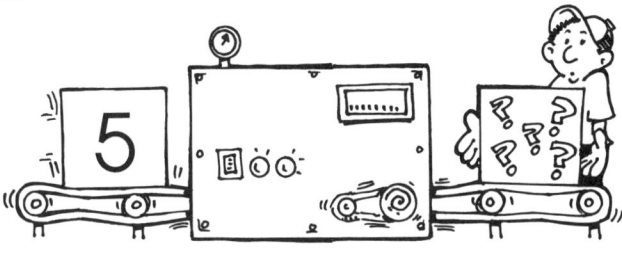

The Magic Number Machine takes 5 away from every number that goes in. If 5 goes in, which number comes out?

(a) 5   (b) 10   (c) 0   (d) none of these choices

EXTEND THE THINKING: Write a number sentence that shows what the machine did.

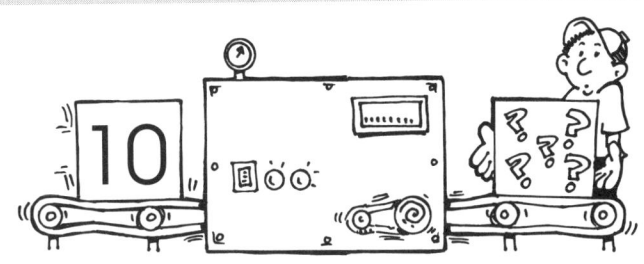

The Magic Number Machine takes 5 away from every number that goes in. If 10 goes in, which number comes out?

(a) 5   (b) 10   (c) 0   (d) none of these choices

EXTEND THE THINKING: Write a number sentence that shows what the machine did.

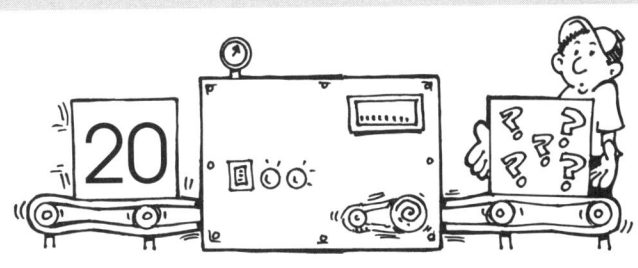

The Magic Number Machine takes 5 away from every number that goes in. If 20 goes in, which number comes out?

(a) 19   (b) 16   (c) 21   (d) none of these choices

EXTEND THE THINKING: Write a number sentence that shows what the machine did.

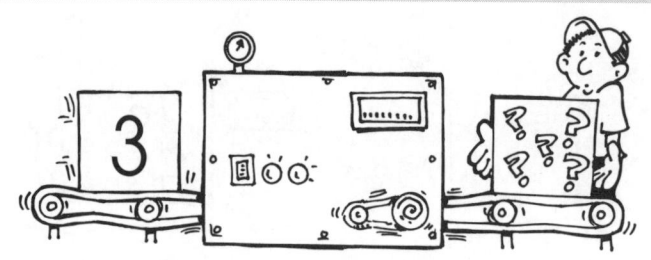

The Magic Number Machine takes 2 away from every number that goes in. If 3 goes in, which number comes out?

(a) 5   (b) 4   (c) 1   (d) none of these choices

EXTEND THE THINKING: Write a number sentence that shows what the machine did.

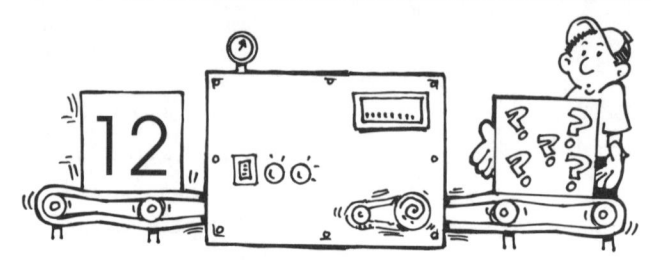

The Magic Number Machine takes 2 away from every number that goes in. If 12 goes in, which number comes out?

(a) 13   (b) 10   (c) 16   (d) none of these choices

EXTEND THE THINKING: Write a number sentence that shows what the machine did.

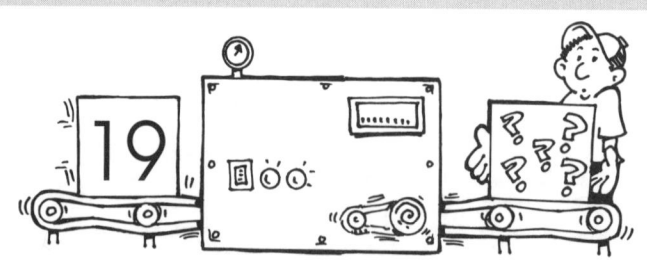

The Magic Number Machine takes 2 away from every number that goes in. If 19 goes in, which number comes out?

(a) 17   (b) 18   (c) 21   (d) none of these choices

EXTEND THE THINKING: Write a number sentence that shows what the machine did.

70 Logic and Critical Thinking

| 2 4 6 |

How are these numbers the same?

ⓐ all odd numbers

ⓑ all even numbers

ⓒ counting by threes

ⓓ none of the above

EXTEND THE THINKING: Which other numbers could go in that group?

| 5 3 7 |

How are these numbers the same?

ⓐ all odd numbers

ⓑ all even numbers

ⓒ counting by fives

ⓓ none of the above

EXTEND THE THINKING: Which other numbers could go in that group?

| 12 16 18 |

How are these numbers the same?

ⓐ all odd numbers

ⓑ all even numbers

ⓒ counting by threes

ⓓ none of the above

EXTEND THE THINKING: Which other numbers could go in that group?

Logic and Critical Thinking

(7   3   9)

How are these numbers the same?

ⓐ all odd numbers

ⓑ all even numbers

ⓒ counting by ones

ⓓ none of the above

EXTEND THE THINKING: Which other numbers could go in that group?

(8   2   4)

How are these numbers the same?

ⓐ all odd numbers

ⓑ all even numbers

ⓒ counting by twos

ⓓ none of the above

EXTEND THE THINKING: Which other numbers could go in that group?

(15   20   25)

How are these numbers the same?

ⓐ all odd numbers

ⓑ all even numbers

ⓒ counting by fives

ⓓ none of the above

EXTEND THE THINKING: Which other numbers could go in that group?

Favorite Pet

How many children said frogs are their favorite pet?

(a) 3   (b) 2   (c) 5   (d) 0

EXTEND THE THINKING: Which pet is more popular?

Favorite Pet

How many children said cats are their favorite pet?

(a) 5   (b) 4   (c) 3   (d) 2

EXTEND THE THINKING: How many children did not choose cats as their favorite pet?

Favorite Pet

Which two animals are the favorite pet of the same number of children?

(a) cats   (b) cats and fish   (c) dogs and fish   (d) dogs and cats

EXTEND THE THINKING: How many kinds of pets are named?

Logic and Critical Thinking 73

Favorite Treat

How many children prefer ice cream?

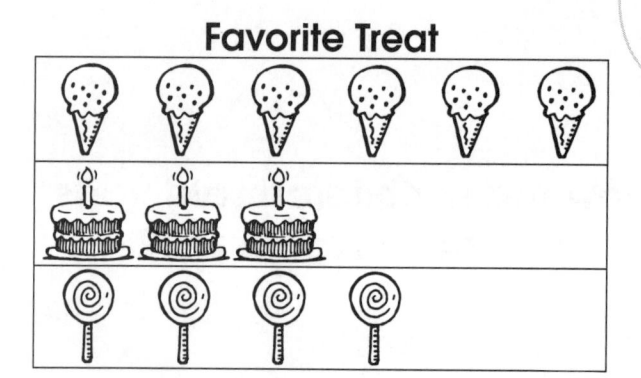

(a) 6 (b) 4 (c) 3 (d) 10

EXTEND THE THINKING: Tell how you solved the problem.

Favorite Treat

How many more children prefer ice cream than children who prefer cake?

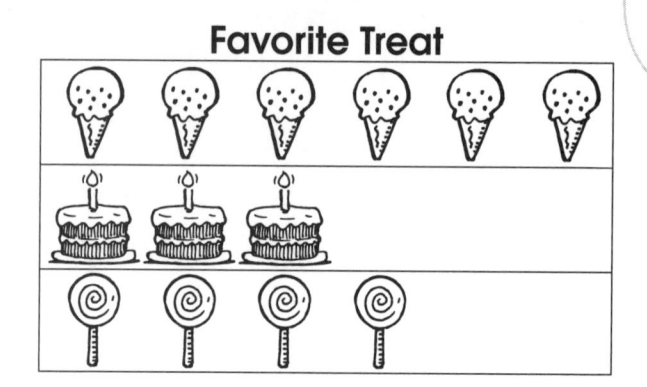

(a) 6 (b) 4 (c) 3 (d) 2

EXTEND THE THINKING: Tell how you solved the problem.

Favorite Treat

How many more children prefer cake or candy than children who prefer ice cream?

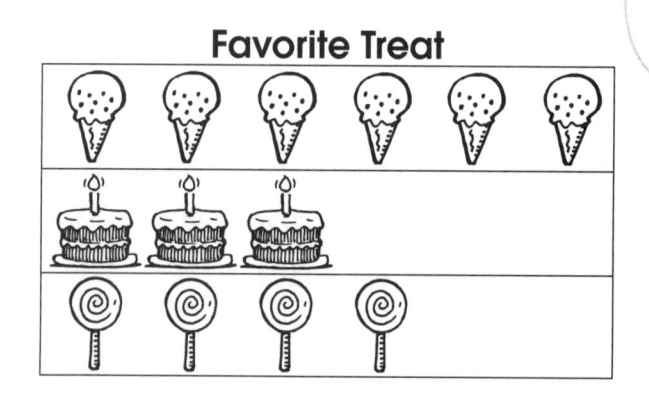

(a) 7 (b) 1 (c) 6 (d) 2

EXTEND THE THINKING: Tell how you solved the problem.

Favorite Sport

How many children prefer soccer?

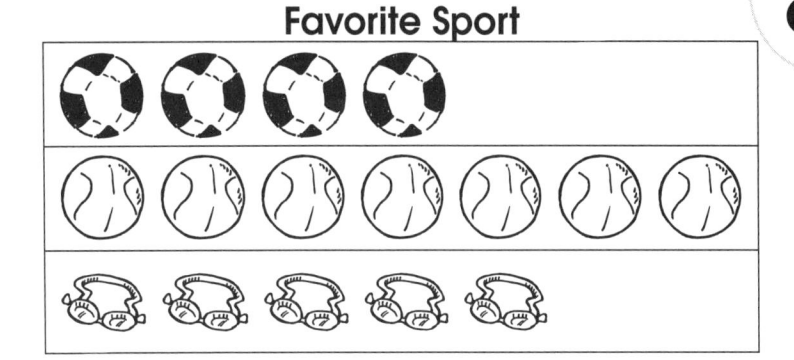

ⓐ 4   ⓑ 6   ⓒ 5   ⓓ 12

EXTEND THE THINKING: Tell how you solved the problem.

Favorite Sport

How many more children prefer basketball than children who prefer soccer?

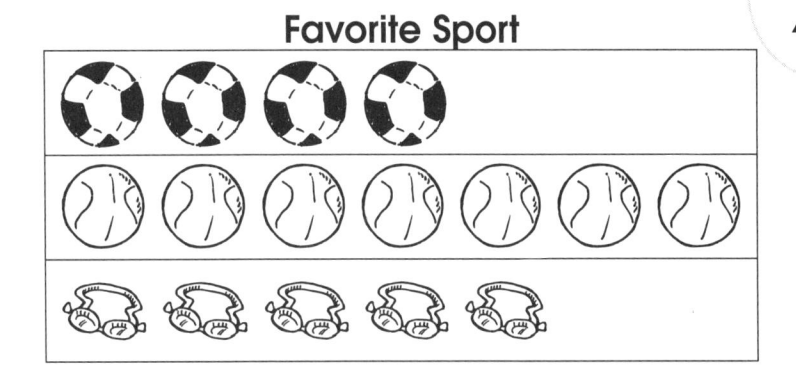

ⓐ 4   ⓑ 6   ⓒ 8   ⓓ 3

EXTEND THE THINKING: Tell how you solved the problem.

Favorite Sport

How many more children prefer soccer or swimming than children who prefer basketball?

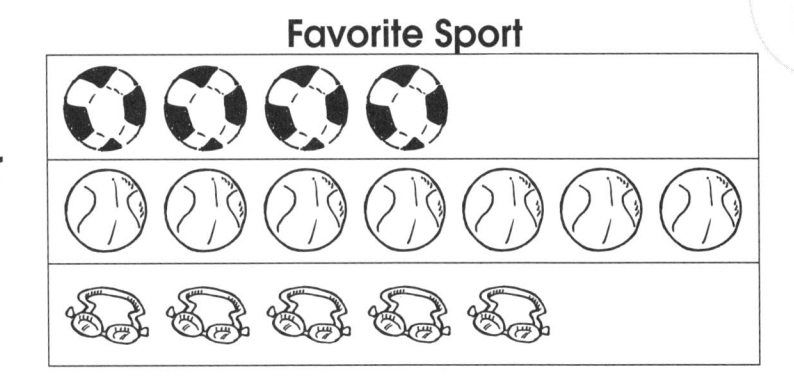

ⓐ 4   ⓑ 7   ⓒ 3   ⓓ 2

EXTEND THE THINKING: Tell how you solved the problem.

Logic and Critical Thinking 75

Section Answers
Logic and Critical Thinking

Correct answers are shaded.

	page 61	page 62	page 63	page 64	page 65
○	ⓐ ⓑ ⓒ **ⓓ**	**ⓐ** ⓑ ⓒ ⓓ	ⓐ **ⓑ** ⓒ ⓓ	ⓐ ⓑ **ⓒ** ⓓ	ⓐ **ⓑ** ⓒ ⓓ
△	**ⓐ** ⓑ ⓒ ⓓ	**ⓐ** ⓑ ⓒ ⓓ	**ⓐ** ⓑ ⓒ ⓓ	**ⓐ** ⓑ ⓒ ⓓ	ⓐ **ⓑ** ⓒ ⓓ
□	**ⓐ** ⓑ ⓒ ⓓ	ⓐ ⓑ **ⓒ** ⓓ	ⓐ ⓑ **ⓒ** ⓓ	ⓐ ⓑ ⓒ **ⓓ**	**ⓐ** ⓑ ⓒ ⓓ

	page 66	page 67	page 68	page 69	page 70
○	ⓐ ⓑ ⓒ **ⓓ**	ⓐ **ⓑ** ⓒ ⓓ	**ⓐ** ⓑ ⓒ ⓓ	ⓐ ⓑ **ⓒ** ⓓ	ⓐ ⓑ **ⓒ** ⓓ
△	ⓐ **ⓑ** ⓒ ⓓ	ⓐ ⓑ **ⓒ** ⓓ	ⓐ ⓑ ⓒ **ⓓ**	ⓐ ⓑ ⓒ **ⓓ**	ⓐ **ⓑ** ⓒ ⓓ
□	**ⓐ** ⓑ ⓒ ⓓ	ⓐ **ⓑ** ⓒ ⓓ	ⓐ ⓑ **ⓒ** ⓓ	ⓐ ⓑ ⓒ **ⓓ**	**ⓐ** ⓑ ⓒ ⓓ

	page 71	page 72	page 73	page 74	page 75
○	ⓐ **ⓑ** ⓒ ⓓ	**ⓐ** ⓑ ⓒ ⓓ	ⓐ **ⓑ** ⓒ ⓓ	**ⓐ** ⓑ ⓒ ⓓ	**ⓐ** ⓑ ⓒ ⓓ
△	**ⓐ** ⓑ ⓒ ⓓ	ⓐ **ⓑ** ⓒ ⓓ	ⓐ **ⓑ** ⓒ ⓓ	ⓐ ⓑ **ⓒ** ⓓ	ⓐ ⓑ ⓒ **ⓓ**
□	ⓐ **ⓑ** ⓒ ⓓ	ⓐ ⓑ **ⓒ** ⓓ	ⓐ ⓑ **ⓒ** ⓓ	ⓐ **ⓑ** ⓒ ⓓ	ⓐ ⓑ ⓒ **ⓓ**

Measurement

The *Level A* Measurement standards require children to

- identify when to use each form of measurement (e.g., inch, cup, pound, minute)
- tell time and identify a time before and after a given time
- estimate measurements that are standard (e.g., inches) and nonstandard (e.g., chocolate squares)
- compare size, weight, height, and capacity
- apply concepts of measurement to real life
- identify coins and count money

Measurement Station

Place various measurement tools (e.g., thermometers, cups, teaspoons, watch) at a measurement station, and invite children to compare and contrast the items. Each week, change the materials at the station. For a group lesson, divide the class into two groups, and give each child in one group a measurement tool. Write on sentence strips what the tools are used to measure, and give each child in the other group a sentence strip. Challenge children to find their partner before you ring a bell. Then, when each child with a measurement tool is paired with the child who has the matching description, ask each pair to stand in front of the class and explain why they go together.

Perimeter Boxes

Give each child one 2" paper square, one 4" paper square, and a ruler. Ask children to compare and contrast the squares and describe what they notice about the two squares. Give each child one 8" and one 16" piece of string. Have children place the string around the perimeter of their squares. Encourage them to make new observations. For a metric lesson, repeat the activity with 5 cm and 10 cm paper squares and 20 cm and 40 cm strings.

TEST-TAKING TIPS FOR CHILDREN

✔ Eat a good breakfast the morning of a test.

✔ Have a healthy snack before a test.

✔ Believe in yourself.

✔ Relax—take a deep breath, and let it out slowly.

TEACHING TIP FOR THIS SECTION

Tell children that one way to solve measurement problems is to color in the pictures. For example, invite children to color in the boxes along the width of the cake in the ● problem on page 83 so that they can see that the correct answer is 5 blocks *(a)*.

➜ Answers are on page 94.

Measurement

Concepts: Measurement

Math Concept	page 79	page 80	page 81	page 82	page 83	page 84	page 85	page 86	page 87	page 88	page 89	page 90	page 91	page 92	page 93
Money	X	X													
Addition	X	X			X		X				X	X			
Time			X	X					X						
Nonstandard Measurement					X	X						X			
Subtraction					X	X		X	X	X					
Estimation							X	X							
Perimeter										X	X				
Area												X	X		
Standard Measurement											X			X	X

78 *Measurement*

You have the most of which coin?

(a) pennies   (b) nickels   (c) dimes   (d) quarters

EXTEND THE THINKING: You have the least of which coin?

How much money do you have altogether?

(a) 25¢   (b) 4¢   (c) 3¢   (d) 8¢

EXTEND THE THINKING: Are your coins worth more than or less than the value of a dime? Tell why.

If you had 2 more pennies, how much money would you have?

(a) 8¢   (b) 10¢   (c) 2¢   (d) 6¢

EXTEND THE THINKING: Which different set of coins would equal the same amount of money?

Measurement

What are the names of these coins?

ⓐ dimes and pennies

ⓑ nickels and pennies

ⓒ dimes and nickels

ⓓ quarters and pennies

EXTEND THE THINKING: What is the value of a dime?

How much money are these coins worth altogether?

ⓐ 25¢   ⓑ 22¢   ⓒ 20¢   ⓓ 2¢

EXTEND THE THINKING: Are the coins worth more than or less than the value of one dime?

If you had 3 more pennies, how much money would you have?

ⓐ 25¢   ⓑ 16¢   ⓒ 3¢   ⓓ 8¢

EXTEND THE THINKING: Which different set of coins would equal the same amount of money?

80 *Measurement*

What time is it?

ⓐ 12:00   ⓑ 7:00   ⓒ 9:00   ⓓ 3:00

EXTEND THE THINKING: What time will it be in 1 hour?

What time is it?

ⓐ 3:30   ⓑ 7:30   ⓒ 3:00   ⓓ 6:30

EXTEND THE THINKING: What time will it be in a half hour?

What time is it?

ⓐ 6:00   ⓑ 3:15   ⓒ 6:15   ⓓ 3:30

EXTEND THE THINKING: What time will it be in 15 minutes?

Measurement 81

What time is it?

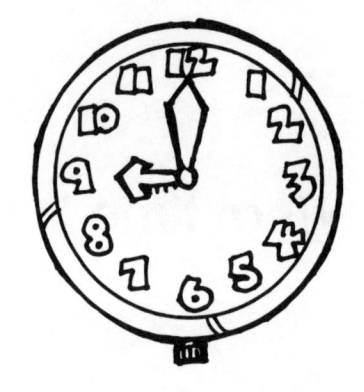

ⓐ 12:00 ⓑ 9:00 ⓒ 6:00 ⓓ 3:00

EXTEND THE THINKING: What time will it be in a half hour?

What time is it?

ⓐ 9:00 ⓑ 7:30 ⓒ 9:30 ⓓ 6:30

EXTEND THE THINKING: What time will it be in 15 minutes?

What time is it?

ⓐ 6:45 ⓑ 3:15 ⓒ 6:15 ⓓ 9:30

EXTEND THE THINKING: What time will it be in 1 hour and 15 minutes?

How wide is the cake?

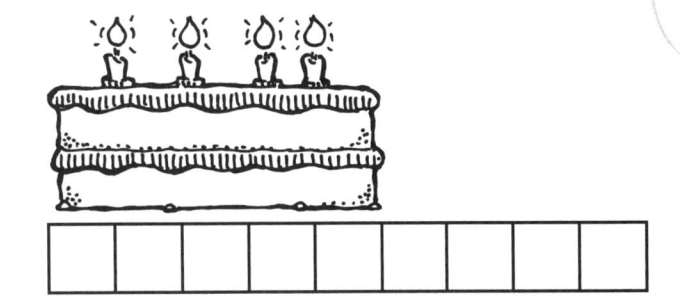

ⓐ 5 blocks   ⓑ 2 blocks   ⓒ 6 blocks   ⓓ 1 block

EXTEND THE THINKING: How wide is your thumbnail?

How much wider is the cake than the cupcake?

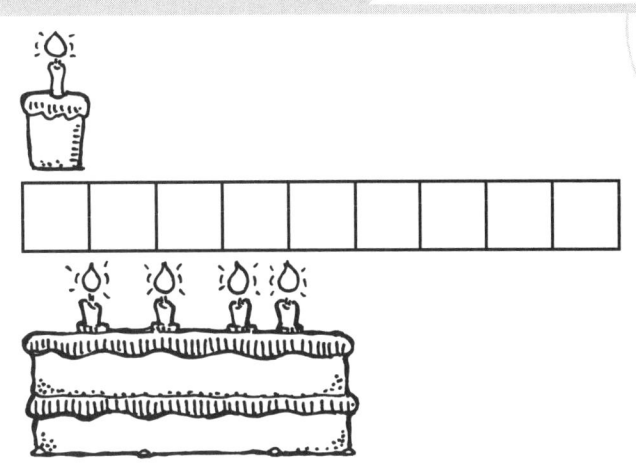

ⓐ 1 block   ⓑ 5 blocks   ⓒ 4 blocks   ⓓ 3 blocks

EXTEND THE THINKING: Which is wider: 3 cupcakes or 1 cake? Tell why.

How wide are two cakes?

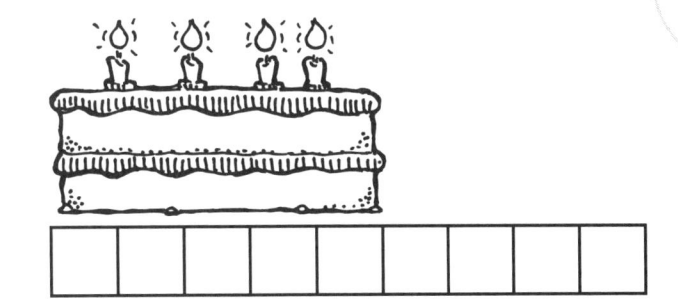

ⓐ 4 blocks   ⓑ 5 blocks   ⓒ 2 blocks   ⓓ 10 blocks

EXTEND THE THINKING: How many cakes fit next to 15 blocks? Tell why.

Measurement

How tall is the giraffe?

ⓐ 3 blocks **ⓑ** 2 blocks **ⓒ** 6 blocks **ⓓ** 4 blocks

EXTEND THE THINKING: How tall is your pencil eraser?

How much taller is the giraffe than the rabbit?

ⓐ 1 block **ⓑ** 2 blocks **ⓒ** 3 blocks **ⓓ** 4 blocks

EXTEND THE THINKING: How many rabbits are as tall as the giraffe? Tell why.

How much shorter is the giraffe than the tree?

ⓐ 1 block **ⓑ** 2 blocks **ⓒ** 3 blocks **ⓓ** 4 blocks

EXTEND THE THINKING: How many blocks do you need to measure 2 trees? Tell why.

A ▭   B ▭

Box A holds 5 cupcakes. How many cupcakes do you estimate Box B holds?

(a) 10   (b) 5   (c) 25   (d) 2

EXTEND THE THINKING: How many cupcakes can both boxes hold?

A ▭   B ▭

Box A holds 20 erasers. How many erasers do you estimate Box B holds?

(a) 10   (b) 20   (c) 25   (d) 40

EXTEND THE THINKING: How many erasers would you have if both boxes were filled?

A ▭   B ▭

Box A holds 50 marbles. How many marbles do you estimate Box B holds?

(a) 10   (b) 50   (c) 100   (d) 25

EXTEND THE THINKING: How many marbles would you have if both boxes were filled?

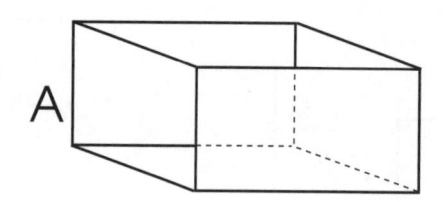

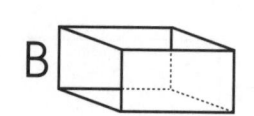

Aquarium A holds 10 fish. How many fish do you estimate Aquarium B holds?

ⓐ 10   ⓑ 5   ⓒ 20   ⓓ 1

EXTEND THE THINKING: How many fish can both aquariums hold?

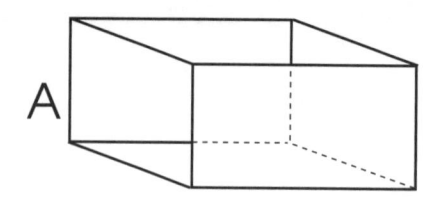

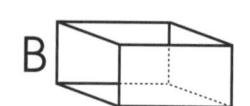

Aquarium A holds 20 fish. How many fish do you estimate Aquarium B holds?

ⓐ 25   ⓑ 20   ⓒ 10   ⓓ 3

EXTEND THE THINKING: How many fish can both aquariums hold?

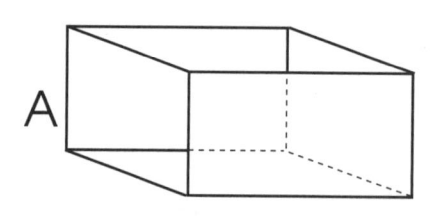

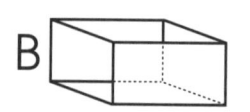

Aquarium A holds 50 fish. How many fish do you estimate Aquarium B holds?

ⓐ 50   ⓑ 25   ⓒ 60   ⓓ 10

EXTEND THE THINKING: How many fish can both aquariums hold?

86 Measurement

Mrs. Jones's class timed how fast their pet rabbit could hop across the room. If the rabbit started at 9:30 and finished at 9:45, how long did it take?

ⓐ 5 minutes　　ⓑ 5 hours　　ⓒ 15 minutes　　ⓓ 15 hours

EXTEND THE THINKING: If the rabbit started at 9:40 and crosses the room in 10 minutes, when would it finish?

Mrs. Jones's class timed how fast their pet rabbit could hop across the hall. If the rabbit started at 9:30 and finished at 9:35, how long did it take?

ⓐ 5 minutes　　ⓑ 5 hours　　ⓒ 30 minutes　　ⓓ 30 hours

EXTEND THE THINKING: If the rabbit started at 9:40 and crosses the hall in 15 minutes, when would it finish?

Mrs. Jones's class timed how fast their pet rabbit could hop across the rug. If the rabbit started at 9:30 and finished at 9:37, how long did it take?

ⓐ 7 minutes　　ⓑ 17 minutes　　ⓒ 5 minutes　　ⓓ 15 minutes

EXTEND THE THINKING: If the rabbit started at 9:45 and crosses the rug in 8 minutes, when would it finish?

Measurement　87

Cookie A is twice the size of Cookie B.
If 10 chocolate chips fit around the edge of Cookie A,
how many chips fit around the edge of Cookie B?

(a) 10   (b) 20   (c) 2   (d) 5

EXTEND THE THINKING: Tell how much smaller Cookie B is than Cookie A.

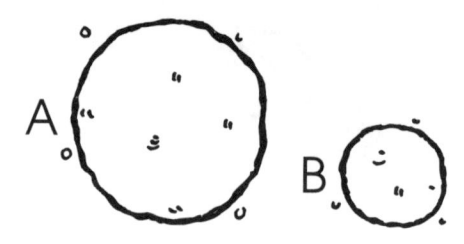

Cookie A is twice the size of Cookie B.
If the perimeter of Cookie A is 20 chocolate chips,
what is the perimeter of Cookie B?

(a) 10 chocolate chips   (b) 20 chocolate chips   (c) 25 chocolate chips   (d) 2 chocolate chips

EXTEND THE THINKING: Tell how you solved the problem.

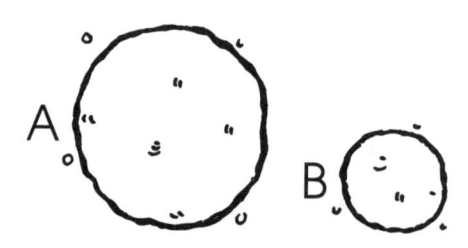

Cookie A is twice the size of Cookie B.
If the perimeter of Cookie A is 34 chocolate chips,
what is the perimeter of Cookie B?

(a) 33 chocolate chips   (b) 36 chocolate chips   (c) 17 chocolate chips   (d) 5 chocolate chips

EXTEND THE THINKING: If Cookie B is the same size as Cookie A, what is the perimeter of Cookie B?

88   Measurement

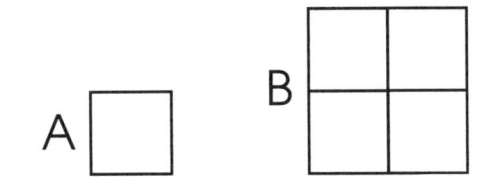

A ☐   B ☐☐

If the perimeter of Box A is 4 inches, what is the perimeter of Box B?

(a) 15 inches (b) 8 inches (c) 6 feet (d) 4 inches

EXTEND THE THINKING: How much bigger would Box B be than Box A? Tell why.

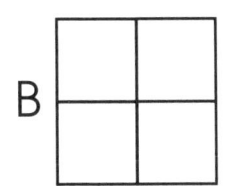

A ☐   B ☐☐

If the perimeter of Box A is 12 inches, what is the perimeter of Box B?

(a) 10 inches (b) 9 inches (c) 5 inches (d) 24 inches

EXTEND THE THINKING: Tell how you solved the problem.

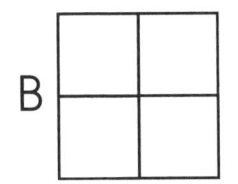

A ☐   B ☐☐

If the perimeter of Box A is 16 inches, what is perimeter of Box B?

(a) 15 inches (b) 3 inches (c) 32 inches (d) 17 inches

EXTEND THE THINKING: If Box B is the same size as Box A, what is the perimeter of Box B?

Measurement 89

If the area of Box A is 4 squares, what is the area of Box B?

ⓐ 9 squares   ⓑ 16 squares   ⓒ 12 squares   ⓓ 18 squares

EXTEND THE THINKING: How many squares are in Box B? Tell why.

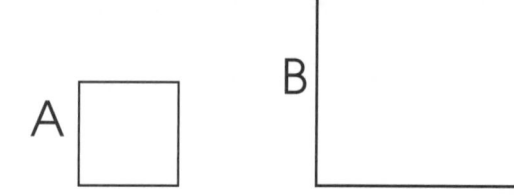

If the area of Box A is 4 squares, what is the area of Box B?

ⓐ 9 squares   ⓑ 12 squares   ⓒ 16 squares   ⓓ 18 squares

EXTEND THE THINKING: Tell how you solved the problem.

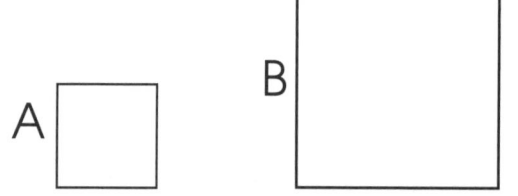

If the area of Box A is 9 squares, what is the area of Box B?

ⓐ 9 squares   ⓑ 36 squares   ⓒ 12 squares   ⓓ 10 squares

EXTEND THE THINKING: If Box B is the same size as Box A, what is the area of Box B?

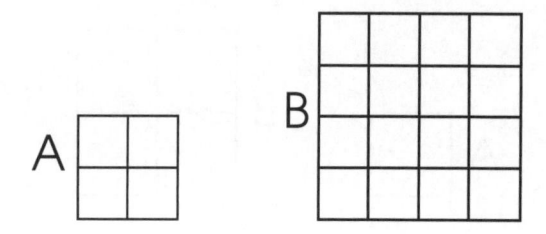

90 *Measurement*

A   B

If the area of Candy Bar A is 10 centimeters, what is the area of Candy Bar B?

(a) 5 centimeters   (b) 10 centimeters   (c) 12 centimeters   (d) 4 centimeters

EXTEND THE THINKING: Tell how you solved the problem.

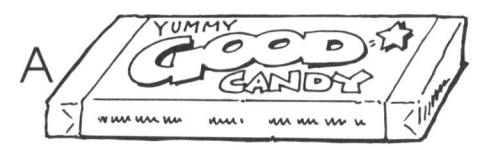

A   B

If the area of Candy Bar A is 20 centimeters, what is the area of Candy Bar B?

(a) 18 centimeters   (b) 22 centimeters   (c) 20 centimeters   (d) 10 centimeters

EXTEND THE THINKING: Tell how you solved the problem.

A   B

If the area of Candy Bar A is 24 centimeters, what is the area of Candy Bar B?

(a) 5 centimeters   (b) 10 centimeters   (c) 12 centimeters   (d) 24 centimeters

EXTEND THE THINKING: Tell how you solved the problem.

Which is the best unit of measurement for figuring out the length of the pencil?

- ⓐ seconds
- ⓑ pounds
- ⓒ minutes
- ⓓ inches

EXTEND THE THINKING: Tell why you made that choice.

Which is the best unit of measurement for figuring out the length of the bat?

- ⓐ seconds
- ⓑ inches
- ⓒ minutes
- ⓓ feet

EXTEND THE THINKING: Tell why you made that choice.

Which is the best unit of measurement for figuring out the length of the eraser?

- ⓐ inches
- ⓑ ounces
- ⓒ feet
- ⓓ seconds

EXTEND THE THINKING: Tell why you made that choice.

Which is the best unit of measurement for figuring out how long it takes a cup of hot water to get cold?

(a) seconds   (b) kilograms   (c) minutes   (d) centimeters

EXTEND THE THINKING: Tell why you made that choice.

Which is the best unit of measurement for figuring out how long it takes for a piece of bread to get moldy?

(a) seconds   (b) years   (c) minutes   (d) days

EXTEND THE THINKING: Tell why you made that choice.

Which is the best unit of measurement for figuring out how long it is until your next birthday?

(a) centimeters   (b) days   (c) years   (d) minutes

EXTEND THE THINKING: Tell why you made that choice.

Measurement 93

Section Answers
Measurement

Correct answers are shaded.

	page 79	page 80	page 81	page 82	page 83
○	**a** b c d	**a** b c d	a b c **d**	a **b** c d	**a** b c d
△	a b c **d**	a **b** c d	**a** b c d	a b **c** d	a b **c** d
□	a **b** c d	**a** b c d	a b **c** d	**a** b c d	a b c **d**

	page 84	page 85	page 86	page 87	page 88
○	a b c **d**	**a** b c d	a **b** c d	a b **c** d	a b c **d**
△	a b **c** d	a b c **d**	a b **c** d	**a** b c d	**a** b c d
□	**a** b c d	a b **c** d	a **b** c d	**a** b c d	a b **c** d

	page 89	page 90	page 91	page 92	page 93
○	a **b** c d	a **b** c d	**a** b c d	a b c **d**	a b **c** d
△	a b c **d**	a b **c** d	a b c **d**	a b c **d**	a b c **d**
□	a b **c** d	a **b** c d	a b c **d**	**a** b c d	a **b** c d

Mathematical Reasoning

The *Level A* Mathematical Reasoning standards require children to

- use discrete math—determine the total number of different ways in which shapes, objects, and numbers can be arranged

- use analogies—compare and contrast shapes, solids, or numbers; examine attributes; and apply basic math skills to discover the relationship between geometric and numerical pairs

- use problem-solving skills—apply basic math concepts to real-life situations

Color Order

Cut out for each child 18 circles, six from red construction paper, six from blue, and six from green. Ask children to make a row that has one circle of each color. Then, have them continue making new rows with three different-colored circles in different orders. If children have difficulty with the activity, have them leave one circle in the same place and switch the other two circles. They can repeat this process by leaving a different circle untouched while they switch the remaining two circles.

Circle-Time Analogies

Use attribute blocks or number cards to create analogies on a magnetic board. Display the attribute blocks or number cards, teach the concept, and invite children to solve the analogies in pairs or small groups. Discuss the solution as a class (e.g., small blue square is to big blue square as small red circle is to big red circle). When using numbers, encourage children to list the ways the two numbers are related before they look at the second set of numbers and the answer choices.

> "6 is to 8 as 4 is to ___.
> 6 and 8 are even numbers.
> 8 is equal to 6+2.

TEST-TAKING TIPS FOR CHILDREN

✔ Look at the choices before reading the questions so you know what to look for.

✔ Read the question. Read every answer before you make your choice.

✔ Check your work. Reread the question and your chosen answer.

TEACHING TIP FOR THIS SECTION

Remind children that sometimes there may be more than one answer to a problem. For example, some children may recognize that in the ● problem on page 104, 4 is 2 more than 2 as well as twice 2. Both 6 (2 more than 4) and 8 (twice 4) are correct answers to this problem. However, 6 is not in the answer choices, so the answer is 8 *(d)*.

→ Answers are on page 112.

Mathematical Reasoning **95**

Concepts: Mathematical Reasoning

Math Concept	page 97	page 98	page 99	page 100	page 101	page 102	page 103	page 104	page 105	page 106	page 107	page 108	page 109	page 110	page 111
Discrete Math	X	X	X	X	X										
Analogies						X	X	X	X	X					
Problem Solving											X	X	X	X	X
Shapes/Solids				X		X	X								
Tally Chart											X	X			
Greater Than/Less Than/Equal To													X	X	
Calendar															X

96 *Mathematical Reasoning*

Rule 1: There are 3 different animals.
Rule 2: Each row can only have one of each animal.

Which row follows these rules?

ⓐ dog, cat, pig
ⓑ cat, cat, pig
ⓒ pig, cat, cat
ⓓ all of the above

EXTEND THE THINKING: Draw the animals in a different order.

Rule 1: There are 3 different animals.
Rule 2: Each row can only have one of each animal.

Which row follows these rules?

ⓐ dog, dog, pig
ⓑ pig, pig, cat
ⓒ cat, pig, dog
ⓓ all of the above

EXTEND THE THINKING: Which rows do not follow the rules? Tell why.

Rule 1: There are 3 different animals.
Rule 2: Each row can only have one of each animal.

Which row follows these rules?

ⓐ dog, pig, cat
ⓑ dog, cat, pig
ⓒ pig, dog, cat
ⓓ all of the above

EXTEND THE THINKING: Draw all the possible ways to arrange the animals.

Mathematical Reasoning

You have 1 cookie, 1 brownie, and 1 doughnut to eat in the next 3 days. In what order could you eat the desserts?

ⓐ cookie, brownie, doughnut

ⓑ brownie, brownie, cookie

ⓒ cookie, cookie, cookie

ⓓ all of the above

EXTEND THE THINKING: Draw another way to eat the desserts.

You have 1 cookie, 1 brownie, and 1 doughnut to eat in the next 3 days. In what order could you eat the desserts?

ⓐ cookie, brownie, doughnut

ⓑ brownie, cookie, doughnut

ⓒ doughnut, brownie, cookie

ⓓ all of the above

EXTEND THE THINKING: Draw two more ways to eat the desserts.

You have 1 cookie, 1 brownie, and 1 doughnut to eat in the next 3 days. In what order could you eat the desserts?

ⓐ cookie, brownie, doughnut

ⓑ cookie, doughnut, brownie

ⓒ brownie, cookie, doughnut

ⓓ all of the above

EXTEND THE THINKING: Draw all the ways to eat the desserts.

98 *Mathematical Reasoning*

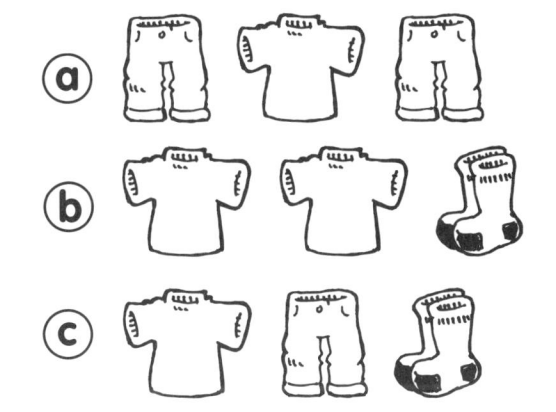

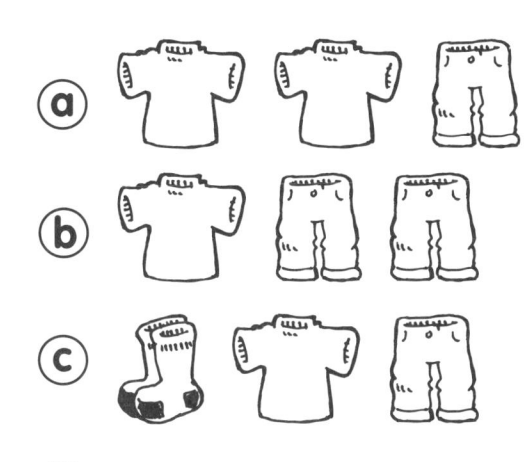

It is time to get dressed. In what order could you put on your shirt, pants, and socks?

ⓐ pants, shirt, pants
ⓑ shirt, shirt, socks
ⓒ shirt, pants, socks
ⓓ all of the above

EXTEND THE THINKING: In what other order can you get dressed?

It is time to get dressed. In what order could you put on your shirt, pants, and socks?

ⓐ shirt, shirt, pants
ⓑ shirt, pants, pants
ⓒ socks, shirt, pants
ⓓ all of the above

EXTEND THE THINKING: In what other order can you get dressed?

It is time to get dressed. In what order could you put on your shirt, pants, and socks?

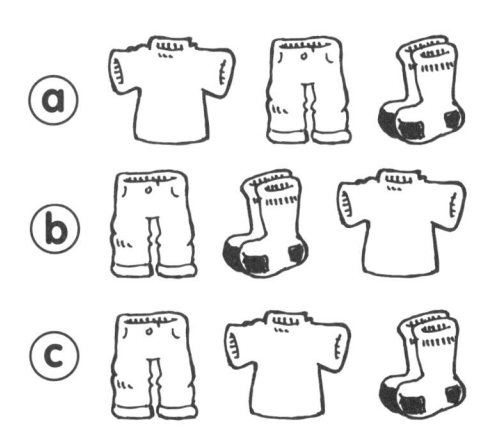

ⓐ shirt, pants, socks
ⓑ pants, socks, shirt
ⓒ pants, shirt, socks
ⓓ all of the above

EXTEND THE THINKING: In what other order can you get dressed?

Mathematical Reasoning 99

Rule 1: There are 3 different shapes.
Rule 2: Each row can have only one of each shape.

Which row follows these rules?

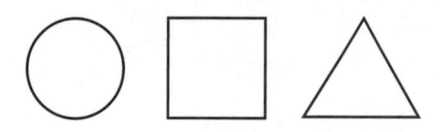

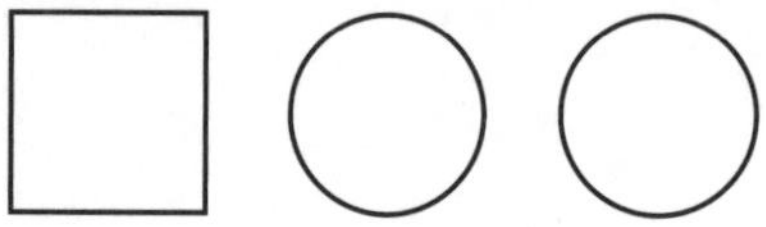

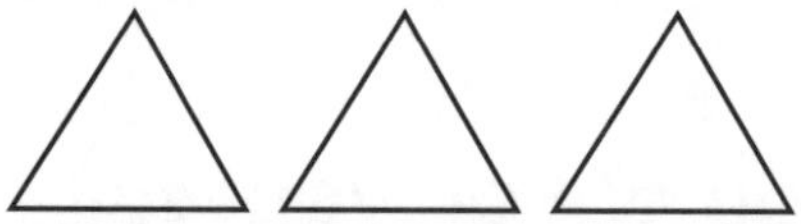

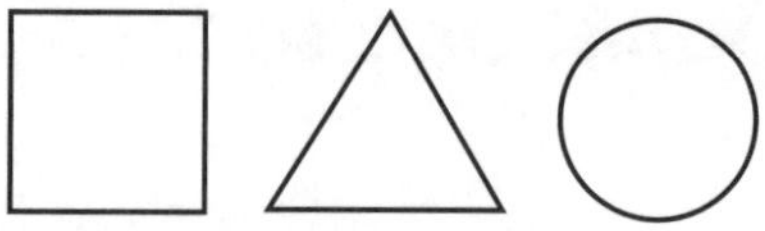

○ □ △

ⓐ □ ○ ○
ⓑ △ △ △
ⓒ □ △ ○
ⓓ all of the above

EXTEND THE THINKING: Draw the shapes in a different order.

Rule 1: There are 3 different shapes.
Rule 2: Each row can have only one of each shape.

Which row follows these rules?

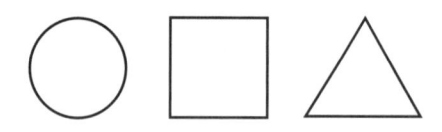

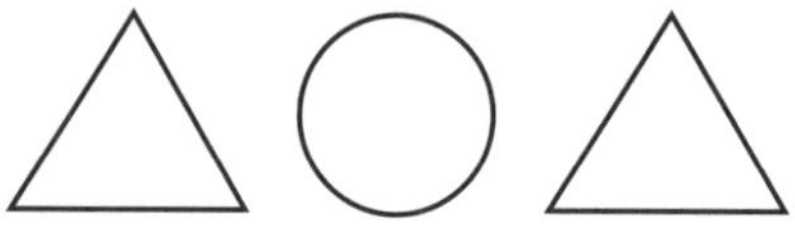

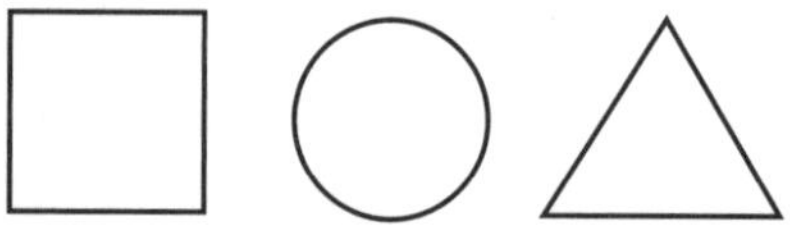

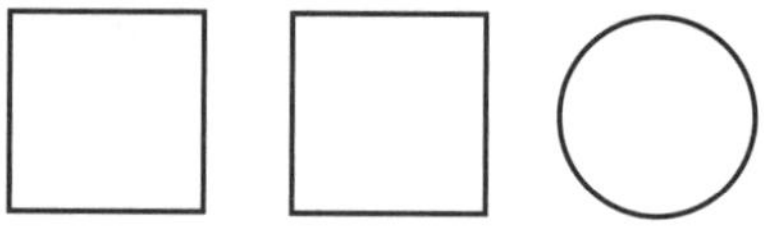

○ □ △

ⓐ △ ○ △
ⓑ □ ○ △
ⓒ □ □ ○
ⓓ all of the above

EXTEND THE THINKING: Which rows don't follow the rules? Tell why.

Rule 1: There are 3 different shapes.
Rule 2: Each row can have only one of each shape.

Which row follows these rules?

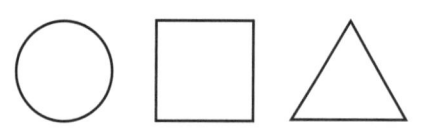

○ □ △

ⓐ △ ○ □
ⓑ □ △ △
ⓒ ○ □ ○
ⓓ all of the above

EXTEND THE THINKING: Draw all the possible ways to arrange the shapes.

100 *Mathematical Reasoning*

Rule 1: There are 3 different blocks.
Rule 2: Each row can have only one of each block.

Which row follows these rules?

ⓐ
ⓑ
ⓒ
ⓓ all of the above

EXTEND THE THINKING: Draw the blocks in a different order.

Rule 1: There are 3 different blocks.
Rule 2: Each row can have only one of each block.

Which row follows these rules?

ⓐ
ⓑ
ⓒ
ⓓ all of the above

EXTEND THE THINKING: Which rows don't follow the rules? Tell why.

Rule 1: There are 3 different blocks.
Rule 2: Each row can have only one of each block.

Which row follows these rules?

ⓐ
ⓑ
ⓒ
ⓓ all of the above

EXTEND THE THINKING: Draw all the possible ways to arrange the blocks.

Mathematical Reasoning 101

☐ is like ☐ as ◯ is like _____

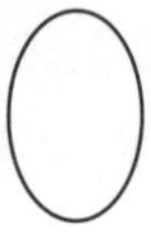

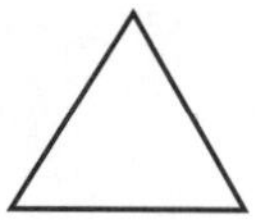

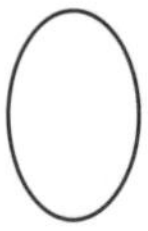

ⓐ △   ⓑ ☐   ⓒ ◯   ⓓ none of these choices

EXTEND THE THINKING: Tell why you made that choice.

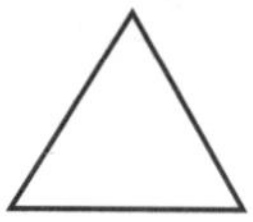

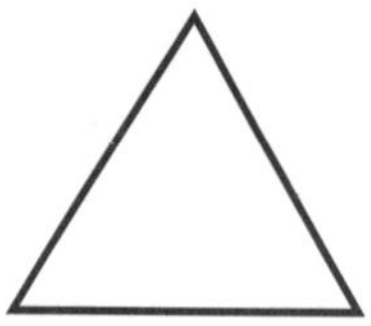

△ is like △ as ☐ is like _____

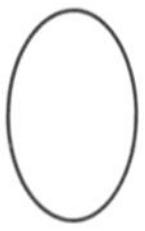

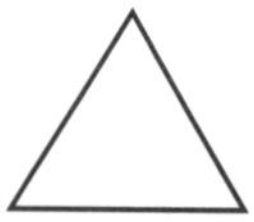

ⓐ ☐   ⓑ ◯   ⓒ △   ⓓ none of these choices

EXTEND THE THINKING: Tell why you made that choice.

▽ is like △ as 🌸 is like _____

ⓐ 🌸   ⓑ △   ⓒ 🌸   ⓓ none of these choices

EXTEND THE THINKING: Tell why you made that choice.

102 *Mathematical Reasoning*

△ is like ▽ as 🐚 is like _____

ⓐ △   ⓑ 🐚   ⓒ ▽   ⓓ none of these choices

EXTEND THE THINKING: Tell why you made that choice.

□ is like ▢ as ○ is like _____

ⓐ ○   ⓑ □   ⓒ ○   ⓓ none of these choices

EXTEND THE THINKING: Tell why you made that choice.

□ is like ◇ as ▭ is like _____

ⓐ ▯   ⓑ ⬡   ⓒ ◇   ⓓ none of these choices

EXTEND THE THINKING: Draw a set of 2 more shapes that fit the analogy.

Mathematical Reasoning 103

2 is to 4   as   4 is to ___

ⓐ 1   ⓑ 4   ⓒ 3   ⓓ 8

EXTEND THE THINKING: Tell why you made that choice.

3 is to 9   as   5 is to ___

ⓐ 1   ⓑ 15   ⓒ 2   ⓓ 10

EXTEND THE THINKING: Tell why you made that choice.

1 is to 10   as   2 is to ___

ⓐ 20   ⓑ 10   ⓒ 5   ⓓ 7

EXTEND THE THINKING: Tell why you made that choice.

104   Mathematical Reasoning

9 : 8 as 6 : ___

ⓐ 1   ⓑ 4   ⓒ 3   ⓓ 5

EXTEND THE THINKING: Tell why you made that choice.

10 : 8 as 5 : ___

ⓐ 1   ⓑ 3   ⓒ 2   ⓓ 7

EXTEND THE THINKING: Tell why you made that choice.

10 : 5 as 20 : ___

ⓐ 20   ⓑ 10   ⓒ 5   ⓓ 7

EXTEND THE THINKING: Tell why you made that choice.

Mathematical Reasoning 105

5 : 4   as   9 : ___

(a) 9   (b) 6   (c) 8   (d) 2

EXTEND THE THINKING: Tell why you made that choice.

12 : 10   as   4 : ___

(a) 2   (b) 6   (c) 10   (d) 12

EXTEND THE THINKING: Tell why you made that choice.

30 : 15   as   20 : ___

(a) 20   (b) 10   (c) 40   (d) 7

EXTEND THE THINKING: Tell why you made that choice.

106   Mathematical Reasoning

Favorite Color

Red								
Blue			
Green				
Yellow						

How many children prefer green?

(a) 7   (b) 2   (c) 3   (d) 5

EXTEND THE THINKING: Draw a group of 5 tally marks.

Favorite Color

Red								
Blue			
Green				
Yellow						

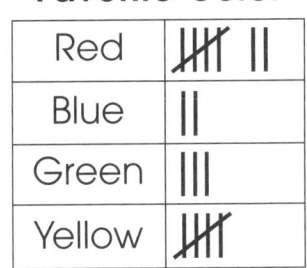

How many more children prefer yellow than green?

(a) 7   (b) 2   (c) 3   (d) 5

EXTEND THE THINKING: Tell how you solved the problem.

Favorite Color

Red								
Blue			
Green				
Yellow						

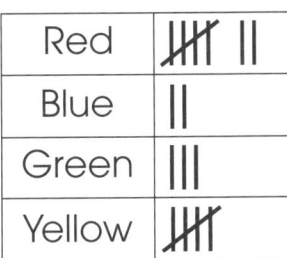

How many more children prefer red than yellow?

(a) 7   (b) 2   (c) 3   (d) 5

EXTEND THE THINKING: Tell how you solved the problem.

Mathematical Reasoning 107

Favorite Game

Tag	卌
Hide-and-Seek	卌 卌
Jump Rope	卌 ||
Four Square	||

How many children prefer Hide-and-Seek?

(a) 5   (b) 10   (c) 7   (d) 2

EXTEND THE THINKING: Draw a group of 10 tally marks.

Favorite Game

Tag	卌
Hide-and-Seek	卌 卌
Jump Rope	卌 ||
Four Square	||

How many more children prefer Jump Rope than Four Square?

(a) 5   (b) 10   (c) 7   (d) 2

EXTEND THE THINKING: Tell how you solved the problem.

Favorite Game

Tag	卌
Hide-and-Seek	卌 卌
Jump Rope	卌 ||
Four Square	||

How many more children prefer Hide-and-Seek than Jump Rope?

(a) 3   (b) 2   (c) 7   (d) 5

EXTEND THE THINKING: Tell how you solved the problem.

○ ○ ○ 3 ◯ 3 ☆ ☆ ☆

Which symbol completes the number sentence?

ⓐ >   ⓑ <   ⓒ =   ⓓ +

EXTEND THE THINKING: If there were 2 more stars, how would that change your answer?

○ ○ 2 ◯ 3 ☆ ☆ ☆

Which symbol completes the number sentence?

ⓐ >   ⓑ <   ⓒ =   ⓓ +

EXTEND THE THINKING: Tell how you solved the problem.

3 ◯ 2

Which symbol completes the number sentence?

ⓐ >   ⓑ <   ⓒ =   ⓓ +

EXTEND THE THINKING: What did you notice about the numbers?

Mathematical Reasoning 109

3 ◯ 2

Which symbol completes the number sentence?

ⓐ >   ⓑ <   ⓒ =   ⓓ +

EXTEND THE THINKING: If there were 2 more presents, how would that change your answer?

4 ◯ 4

Which symbol completes the number sentence?

ⓐ >   ⓑ <   ⓒ =   ⓓ +

EXTEND THE THINKING: Tell how you solved the problem.

5 ◯ 8

Which symbol completes the number sentence?

ⓐ >   ⓑ <   ⓒ =   ⓓ +

EXTEND THE THINKING: What did you notice about the numbers?

110   Mathematical Reasoning

January

S	M	T	W	T	F	S
	1	2	3	4	5	6
7	8	9	10	11	12	13
14	15	16	17	18	19	20
21	22	23	24	25	26	27
28	29	30	31			

How many days are there in the month shown?

(a) 28   (b) 29   (c) 30   (d) 31

EXTEND THE THINKING: Which month is shown?

November

S	M	T	W	T	F	S
				1	2	3
4	5	6	7	8	9	10	11
12	13	14	15	16	17	18
19	20	21	22	23	24	25
26	27	28	29	30		

Which day of the week is November 22?

(a) Monday   (b) Tuesday   (c) Wednesday   (d) Thursday

EXTEND THE THINKING: Which day of the week is November 23?

July

S	M	T	W	T	F	S
1	2	3	4	5	6	7
8	9	10	11	12	13	14
15	16	17	18	19	20	21
22	23	24	25	26	27	28
29	30	31				

Which date will it be 2 days after July 13?

(a) July 8   (b) July 15   (c) July 22   (d) August 10

EXTEND THE THINKING: Which day of the week is that day?

Section Answers
Mathematical Reasoning

Correct answers are shaded.

	page 97	page 98	page 99	page 100	page 101
○	a b c **d**	**a** b c d	a b **c** d	a b **c** d	a b c **d**
△	a b **c** d	a b c **d**	a b **c** d	a **b** c d	a **b** c d
□	a b c **d**	a b c **d**	a b c **d**	**a** b c d	a b c **d**

	page 102	page 103	page 104	page 105	page 106
○	a b **c** d	a **b** c d	a b c **d**	a b c **d**	a b **c** d
△	**a** b c d	a b **c** d	a **b** c d	a **b** c d	**a** b c d
□	**a** b c d	**a** b c d	**a** b c d	a **b** c d	a **b** c d

	page 107	page 108	page 109	page 110	page 111
○	a b **c** d	a **b** c d	a b **c** d	**a** b c d	a b c **d**
△	a **b** c d	**a** b c d	a **b** c d	a b **c** d	a b **c** d
□	a **b** c d	**a** b c d	**a** b c d	a **b** c d	a **b** c d

112 Mathematical Reasoning